P9-CBA-668

Once Upon a Lifetime...

BACKTRACKING
through the

50's

Don Doyle, DMin, PhD

Asa HOUSE Books
Memphis, TN
2005

Once Upon a Lifetime...

BackTracking Through the 50's

by

Don Doyle, DMin, PhD
Illustrations by Roe Kienle

Published by:

Asa HOUSE Books
110 Timber Creek Drive
Memphis, TN 38018
901/ 757-2347

All rights reserved. No part of this book may be reproduced or transmitted in any form or by any means, electronic or mechanical, including photocopying, recording or by any information storage and retrieval system without written permission from the author except for the inclusion of brief quotations in a review.

Copyright @ 2005

First Printing 2005

Library of Congress Control Number: 2004113011

Doyle, Don

ISBN 1-928577-05-9

174 Pages

$24.95

About the Author

Since 1966, Dr. Don Doyle has functioned in some official capacity as a psychotherapist, minister, or counselor. In that period of time, he has logged more than 45,000 hours of listening to people from forty-two states and eighteen foreign countries.

With degrees in biology (BS), theology (MDiv and DMin), and marriage and family counseling (PhD), Dr. Doyle brings a varied background to the therapy room. In addition, he was in the pastoral ministry for thirteen years, ten of which was spent in one church.

Prior to entering the ministry, he served as a Naval Aviation Officer. As he puts it, "I joined the Navy to see the world and spent three years in Florida. But the value of my military experience was equal to a post-graduate degree." While serving in the navy, he received special commendation awards from the French, Italian, and Australian navies.

As a popular speaker and lecturer, Dr. Doyle has conducted numerous seminars and conferences and delivered after-dinner speeches all across the country. He speaks to churches, civic clubs, corporations, and counseling centers. In addition, he has made many guest appearances on radio and television.

For eight years, he was Associate Director of the *Burlingame* (California) *Counseling Center*. Since 1987, he has directed the *Doyle Family Counseling Center* in Memphis, Tennessee.

Married since 1963 to Martha Longmire Doyle, they have three children– Matt and Chad Doyle and Leanne Duncan and six grandchildren– Brady, and Ellie Doyle, Austin, Bryce, Colby, and Tyler Duncan.

Also by Don Doyle

Heroes of the Heart

Change is a Choice

The Courage to Change Your Mind...
Is the Power to Change Your Life

Dedicated
To
Ellen Elizabeth (Ellie) Doyle
Born 11/18/03

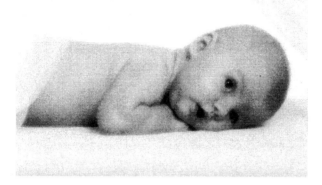

My dear Ellie:

Welcome to our family. We've been waiting for you for a long time. What a treat to have you join us so close to Christmas which makes you a very special Christmas present for us all. Our holiday celebration began on the morning of November 18 when you entered our world safe and sound with all your parts in place. At 6 pounds and 13 ounces, you were a perfect little bundle of joy from the very beginning.

Just in case you don't know, you are the very first granddaughter for Mama D and me. In addition, you are the first granddaughter for your Alexander grandparents, too, which makes you very special to a lot of people. So, no matter what happens from here on out, being "The First Granddaughter" is a title you will carry the rest of your life.

During the last few weeks before you entered this world, you had been giving your mom a hard time. You were doing the normal stuff a late pregnancy child does– kicking, pushing, stretching, and stuff like that– but it was very difficult for your mom to handle. Your dad tried talking to you but it didn't seem to work. So, he sent an email to all the family with an official warning that at the moment you were born, you might immediately be put in "time out!" According to his explanation, that would make sure you didn't get the idea that you could be a defiant child without repercussions.

But here's what happened– when he saw you, you melted his heart and he changed his mind and postponed any "time out" until later. However, it seems that you took that as a sign that you could pretty much have your way with them because during these first five weeks you have indeed been quite defiant. You sleep in the daytime, stay awake at night, and cry until you "get your way." You don't like to be left alone and when you are not being held and rocked and patted, you cry even louder. And when you are in some sort of discomfort like being hungry or having a wet or dirty diaper, you scream your head off. I'm quite sure it's your way of saying that he hurt your feelings when he threatened to give you a timeout at birth and you are making him pay dearly for such a calloused reaction. I think you are saying, "Dad, you think I was defiant before birth– you ain't seen nothing yet!"

Back to more serious stuff. Ellie, you are very fortunate, indeed, because you have a great set of parents and a fine big brother who are going to surround you with affection, attention, and admiration. You should see the way Brady smiles when he tells people about having a little sister. He is so pleased and proud to have you join the family and he can't wait until you are a little older so he can play with you and teach you all sorts of things. On the day of your birth and for a couple of days after, he wore a shirt and a big button that said, "I'm a Big Brother" and when someone asked him about it, he would grin from ear to ear. So, you can be sure that Brady is going to always be there for you to support and protect you– that's pretty special.

Well, that's about it for now. It's Christmas Eve night and we're all here– Uncle Chad and Aunt Heather, Uncle Kelly and Aunt Leanne, cousins Austin and Bryce, your Mom, Dad and big brother Brady, Mama D and Papa, and we're enjoying each other and especially you, our newest family member and very first granddaughter– Ellen Elizabeth Doyle. Welcome to our world.

With much love,

Papa Don   12/24/03

In Memory

of

Dr. Cecil G. Osborne

1904-1999

➤

Who taught me the value of Backtracking
by...

Remembering,
Re-living, (and)
Releasing the past.

Acknowledgments

➤

With gratitude and thanksgiving, I applaud the Parsons High School class of 1959 of which I was honored to be a member. That group was and is a very unique bunch of people. There was a chemistry in that class that bonded us together in a way that created a lifetime of friendships that I truly believe was and is extraordinary.

➤

Special plaudits to Roe Kienle for another superb job with the illustrations. Even though we've worked together on several projects, it's still amazing to me that she can take a rough draft of my writing and draw just the right picture to match the story. Roe has a unique gift and I'm honored that she shares it with me.

➤

Kudos to lifelong friend, Diane Tinker O'Cain, for her invaluable help with editing, proofing, and support. In addition to having an eagle eye for finding errors, Diane also offered excellent suggestions for improving the text.

Introduction

Having reached senior citizen status, I have now fully experienced the three maxims that I've been telling others for years about life: (1) *Time flies whether you're having fun or not.* (2) *Aging is like a roll of toilet paper, the closer you get to the end, the faster it rolls.* (3) *Gravity always wins!*

Now that I'm well into the fourth quarter of the game, I've decided to write a series of books about life as I have experienced and understand it. Starting with childhood (which is the focus of this volume) the additional pieces will be somewhat sequential with some obvious overlaps along the way.

Reflecting on my life, I notice that the majority of the memorable experiences relate to the people I have known– family, friends, business associates, teachers, coaches, clients and total strangers. This series will include all of the above and for the most part will focus on the people who have crossed my path and influenced my life. Sometimes they taught me, sometimes humbled me, sometimes made me laugh, cry, and swear, but always made my life richer and more meaningful. As the title declares, this collection focuses on those fellow travelers who journeyed with me to "the far side of life" during my youth, the time we know as *the 50's.*

Roadmap for Touring the 50's

Prologue

During early January a few years ago, Martha and I spent two weeks in Tucson, AZ, at the Golf Villas at the El Conquistador Country Club in the Oro Valley. The primary purpose for our visit was to see if it would help my respiratory health. Didn't help my health a whole lot but it did my attitude a world of good– primarily because the temperature was in the 70's and one day the humidity actually got up to an obscene high of 18%! Yep, as the Arizonians say, "It's hot but it's dry heat." How dry was it, you ask? In fact, we found it so dry that after getting out of the pool, you had the option of grabbing a towel or just letting nature take care of it for you.

Speaking of the pool– I spent most of my time sitting poolside and reading. My reading material for this trip was: Stephen King's <u>Black House</u>, Rick Bragg's <u>Ava's Man</u>, and astro-physicist, Dr. Stephen Hawking's <u>The Universe in a Nutshell</u>.

As always, I was amazed at the imagination of King and his ability to scare the pants off of you and once again, I loved the story-telling style of Rick Bragg. Reading Stephen Hawking was another story. If I'm real honest with myself and give myself the benefit of the doubt, I probably understood about 10% of what Hawking was saying, but I wanted the other people around the pool to think I was brilliant! So, I'd read Stephen King or Rick Bragg until people started gathering around the pool and then I'd pick up Hawking. With the dust jacket still on, I held it at just the right angle so they could see the title <u>The Universe in a Nutshell</u>. Then I'd watch as they'd punch each other and whisper, "That guy must be a genius!" (Now wipe that high and mighty smirk off your face– don't be acting like you've never done anything for show!)

But seriously folks, the reading of Professor

Hawking's book, <u>The Universe in a Nutshell</u>, intrigued me so much that I put it down and started thinking– *How would I summarize my 35 years and nearly 45,000 hours of listening to people tell their stories? How would I put into a nutshell what I think I've learned about being mentally, emotionally, and spiritually healthy?* I started journaling about it. (See, I not only teach it, I do it!)

After a couple of hours and several pages of free flowing consciousness, I stopped and started culling. When I finished, I was pleasantly surprised with the final draft. To be mentally, emotionally, and spiritually healthy means to live your life– **T**hinking, **F**eeling, and **A**cting with this maxim– are you ready for this?

The Present is not the Past & Today is not Tomorrow

"Say what?" Yes, you heard me correctly. The present is not the past– today is not tomorrow. At this point in my life, that's the best I can do in summarizing the healthy life. Admittedly, this is profoundly simple, but I happen to believe that it's also simply profound. This maxim is the mother-lode in learning to live fully in the here and now by releasing the past and resolving the future.

To celebrate living in the present, you have to deal with yesterday and tomorrow. To squeeze every drop of nectar from the roses of life, you have to let bygones be bygones and come to grips with the great not yet. The past and the future are twin thieves that rob us of today. To celebrate living in the here and now means the present is not the past and today is not tomorrow.

But how do you release the past and resolve the future? The best and most productive method that I have found is to do some *backward thinking* and RELIVE the past by walking through your history page by page, chapter   by chapter, segment by segment.   In so doing, you can heal the hurts and celebrate the joys; you can separate the wheat from the chaff; you can save what is worth saving and with the breath of kindness blow the rest away.

Historian, Daniel Boorstin, warned that *planning for the future without a sense of history is like planting cut flowers.* Without sounding overly dramatic, that, my friend, is what this book is about. But let me give you a forewarning– it's very personal.   It may be too personal for some readers who may surmise that it's self-indulgent and too confessional. Be that as it may. But in telling the story of my youth (as least a portion of it), it's my hope that you will take the bait and also tell your story in written form. If that happens, then I'll count this effort a total success.

➤

A Brief Family History

In order to put things in the proper perspective, it's important to include some pertinent information regarding my family of origin.

Without question, my view of the 50's was greatly influenced by my small Southern home town and the hard-working, straight middle-class, family in which I was reared. As the first-born of four, I certainly carry a lot of the first-born syndrome . My father, Maxie Doyle, was also first-born and so was his mother, Willie Yates Doyle. This first-born lineage meant I was fortunate enough to know my paternal great grandmother, Molly Yates, very well and over an unusual period of time, since she didn't die until I was in college.

My mother, Zula Rhodes Doyle, was the last of nine born to Asa and Fleatie Rhodes. Eight lived to adulthood and all of them had children. To say the least, we were a big bunch. There were 32 of us that made up "the Rhodes first-cousins" all of which emphasizes that I grew-up around a passel of relatives.

When I was born in late '41, my parents were 23 and 18. I've often said to my mother, that she and I "grew up together." My brother, Michael Robert, (soon called Mickey by the family) was born a couple of months after I turned four. My first memory of him is a bit of unpleasant humor and occurred on the day he came home from the hospital which was also the day he was born.

A woman by the name of Mary Cody was a short-term nanny of sorts who would help mothers with newborns for a few days. Miss Mary was changing Mickey's diaper and with great interest I was sitting on the floor watching the whole thing. All at once he shot a pressure packed stream and peed right in my face. I was mortified but Miss Mary, cackling like a banty rooster, helped me to get over being humiliated and prompted me to laugh as well.

Mickey started to school when I began the fifth grade and we walked to school every day, a distance of about ten miles and it was uphill both ways! (Truth be told, I *pulled* him along the 1½ mile trek with nary a hill in sight but that other stuff makes a better story.)

Two months before I turned eight we welcomed dear, sweet, Sheila Ann to our clan. What a treat to have a sister whom I adored from the get-go! Still do. (I'm pretty confident that she liked me okay, too.) Sheila would quickly become the sparkplug in our bunch with energy to burn and enthusiasm for anything and everything.

The 50's was the era of baton twirling and Sheila took to it like a bee takes to honey. I can't remember a time when there wasn't one or more batons either lying around our house or in one of her hands. Before she was old enough to know any better, she was teaching younger girls the fine art of baton twirling and made some good money as the director of "Sheila's Little Strutters."

As a family of five, we motored along pretty well. Our father was a sewing machine mechanic at Salant & Salant, the local garment factory, and our mother was a housewife and homemaker, who also worked at the factory for a while, then worked in a local cloth shop, sold Avon, assisted in a church kindergarten, and eventually bought a women's clothing store.

In the summer before I turned fifteen in the fall, baby brother Christopher Max became the latest addition to our family clan. Having a sibling that much younger gave me a chance for a practice run at being a parent. For three years before I went away to college, Chris and I basically had a parent/child relationship and in all truth has continued from then until now which was/ has been/ and is extremely good for me– I'm not so sure he would say the same. Having two fathers or father figures could get a little irksome, I'm sure.

So, that's the thumbnail version of my immediate and extended family histories– both of which made huge contributions to life as I saw and experienced it while growing up in Parsons, Tennessee, a small rural community in West Tennessee in the time frame which we know as **The 50's**.

Backtracking

In the spring of '99, I was invited to speak to the senior class and to the student body of Riverside High School in Decatur County, Tennessee. Riverside was the result of the merger of Parsons High School and Decaturville High School many years earlier.

Since I was a graduate of Parsons High, I was viewed somewhat as an alumnus of Riverside and due to the fact I had published a couple of books, I was viewed as therefore qualified as a motivator to encourage these young students. It had been many years since I had spoken to a large group of teenagers and, to say the least, it was a sobering experience. In fact, I seriously doubted that anything I said was remembered by any of them for more than a New York minute.

Due to the fact it had been 40 years since I was in high school, I was just too far out of touch to significantly impact their lives. However, that experience was extremely valuable to me because it set in motion an avalanche of memories of my youth. Ironically, three months later, the Parsons High class of '59 observed and somewhat celebrated the 40th anniversary of our high school graduation. It was a little awkward and more than a little scarey to *celebrate* how old "those people" looked; hearing talk of retirement, senior citizen discounts, and AARP! And it was quite clear that most of us were suffering from a severe case of the 5 B's of senior citizenry–baldness, bifocals, bridgework, bulging, and bunions! But, I'm getting ahead of myself...

In anticipation of the reunion, for several days prior to the event, I started thinking about the differences between the class of '99 and the class of '59. In fact, I couldn't stop thinking about it! Since

I'm more than a little obsessive compulsive, the night before the reunion I stayed up until 3:00 a.m. writing about the 50's. Got up at 7:30 and started again. Since then, the process has continued as I've added numerous snippets.

As a result of all this pondering, I read a small portion of what I had written at the reunion, and more than likely overshot my welcome and probably bored my fellow classmates. However, some of them were intrigued enough to encourage me to expand on my thoughts and even suggested that I develop it into

a book. I felt flattered, thought it was an interesting idea, but didn't really imagine that was an option. But time and more obsession brought the concept to fruition. To those who encouraged, I thank you. To those who endured, I thank you, also.

In all of this, you will find one ribbon of continuity– there is an incredible contrast between the 18-year-olds who headed out to become adults at the end of the 20th and beginning of the 21st century and millennium and those of us who set out on the same mission forty or so years ago.

In trying to give this piece a title, I considered: *Reliving the 50's, Remembering the 50's,* and *A Memoir of the 50's,* but each of those sounded too bland. I was tempted to use *The Way We Were* but remembered that had already been taken! I deliberated on *The Way We NEVER Were* thinking that in some ways many of the images of the 50's– especially from old television reruns such as *Ozzie & Harriet, Father Knows Best, Make Room for Daddy*– depict life like it never was. None of us came from families like those. They were mythological and unrealistic. In fact, those shows probably damaged us to the extent they increased our guilt when we did not and could not reproduce such families of our own.

But, be that as it may, I chose the title *Once Upon a Lifetime... Backtracking Through the 50's* because I truly believe this captures best what I want this piece to be– a rumination of my childhood and young adulthood during the time we know as the 50's.

For sure, my reflections on the 50's are nothing new. Strangely enough, those years have generated nostalgic fascination since the early 70's. Perhaps George Lucas was the catalyst with his 1973 blockbuster movie *American Graffiti,* the success of which prompted ABC to re-launch a previous sitcom flop– *Happy Days.* Depicting life in the 50's from American's heartland, Milwaukee, Wisconsin, *Happy Days* aired the second time in 1974 and went on a ten-year run as one of the top television programs of all time. Is that strange, or what?

Why was the American public of the 70's so enamored with life in the 50's that it would make

Happy Days one of the most successful television sitcoms of all time? Doesn't take a genius to figure that out! The assassinations of John F. Kennedy, Martin Luther King, Jr., and Robert F. Kennedy, the Vietnam war, the riots between the war resisters and the war supporters, the Kent State shootings, Watergate, and President Nixon's resignation– all shown daily in living color in nearly every household in the country– left America desperately primed and gasping for some believable signs of Happy Days.

Since the future looked about as promising as a straw hut in a hurricane, the only hopeful look was backwards. So, through the magic of media, America leapfrogged rearward over the turbulent, chaotic, cold 60's to the peaceful, passive, warm 50's when life was like–

Summertime and the living is easy, fish are jumping
and the cotton is high, your daddy's rich and your
momma's good looking, so hush little baby, don't you cry.

The success of reliving the 50's lifestyle through *Happy Days* prompted spinoffs that also had successful runs– *Laverne and Shirley*, and if you can believe this, the tremendously popular *Mork and Mindy*, (which launched the incredible career of Robin Williams) was a spinoff of an episode of Happy Days when an alien from planet Ork attempted to kidnap Richie.

The list could go on and on, right up to the present as Public Television continues to air hugely successful musical tributes to Rock and Roll and Doo Wop which was music centered squarely in the 50's. In addition, Bill Gaither has been extremely successful in reviving 50's style Southern gospel music in his series of *Reunions and Homecomings* that feature legendary gospel singers who were in their heyday during the 50's.

The entertainment media's fascination with the 50's didn't stop with television programming. Steven Spielberg's 1985 huge box-office success, *Back to the Future*, also took us once again to the 50's.

Yes, my intrigue with the 50's has indeed been shared by numerous others through all sorts of media. However, the authenticity of this offering is simply that these reflections are based solely on my own personal experiences in Parsons, a small rural town in Decatur County, Tennessee. But the setting could have been AnySmallTown, USA, and is applicable to anyone who grew up with a sense of "community" whether in housing projects, neighborhoods from metropolitan areas, or small towns. As Don Henley put it so succinctly— *Somewhere back there in the dust, that same small town is in each of us.*

➤

One of the primary reasons I decided to publish this piece is the hope that in sharing memories of my "small town" you will be motivated to write memories of your "small town." Again, small town is any place that provided a sense of "community" whether it was in a rural farming area, an inner city housing project, or an affluent neighborhood in a metropolitan area. Wherever you "belonged" is your small town and trying your hand at writing your memories about it, including the good, the bad, and the ugly, will surprise you on at least three levels— (1) how much you will remember once you start; (2) how emotional you will be after getting into the flow of it; (3) and how therapeutic it will become as your story unfolds. If you'll try it, I can almost guarantee you're going to like it.

Let me add one disclaimer. Right from the get-go, I want to put the quietus on any notion that I'm depicting the 50's as better than the present. I'm not saying those were the good old days in contrast to these being the bad old days. I'm not idolizing the 50's nor denigrating the decades that followed, including the current one. I'm not trying to say that kids today have had life easier or have been pampered, spoiled, and sheltered. I think this is a terrific time to be starting adult life.

What I am trying to convey in this offering is simply this— *life was quite different back then than it is now.* Make no mistake about it, life today is strikingly unlike it was in the 50's— different enough to be mind boggling. Of that I am sure!

Okay, I will confess to one overwhelming fantasy. Oh what I would give to slip back into the 50's for one summer, one month, or even one week, with my kids and their kids! I would love to show them the people, places, and things of my youth. How I wish I could go back in time and share the 50's with the children of the 70's, 80's, 90's and the present. Yeah, I'd like that a lot. Wouldn't you?!

The 50's...

A Place in Time or a State of Mind?

I wish a buck was still silver, and it was back
When the country was strong.
Back before Elvis & the Vietnam war came along.
Before the Beatles and yesterday,
When a man could still work and still would.
...is the best of the free life behind us now

Are the good times really over for good?

I wish coke was still cola,
And a joint was a bad place to be.
It was back before Nixon lied to us all on t.v.
Before microwave ovens,
And a girl could still cook and still would
...is the best of the free life behind us now

Are the good times really over for good?

Merle Haggard

For those of us who lived in the 50's, Merle Haggard's song, *Are The Good Times Really Over For Good* paints a clear picture of life in that era. No doubt some of these lyrics are chauvinist, sexist, and dated. But they do, without question, depict life as it was in that period.

Remembering the 50's brings thoughts of peace, prosperity, and productivity. It's usually referred to as the best of times in American culture; the post-War II period when America got back on track in life, living, and the pursuit of happiness.

Even though the Korean War occurred during this period, it truly is the "forgotten war" in our history. Due to the American people's adverse reaction to entering another war, Korea was generally explained and dismissed as only "a police action." Although this was total propaganda, it insulated the public, particularly the voters, from being distracted in their pursuit of the emerging "happy ever after" dream. So, a reference to the 50's in American history usually means *the best of the best of times.* And without question, it was a great time to grow up. However, this time frame was also filled with many tragedies, heartaches, and national shame.

This offering is not a carefully researched piece of history, rather, it's the story of one man's memory. So strap on your seatbelt and ride along with me on a sentimental journey as I reminisce about what I remember about the 50's including the good, the bad, and the ugly. As a card carrying clinical member of that era, the authenticity of my story is quite simple— from start to finish, I was there!

Just Remembering

The 50's was the "Era of the Car" when cars were works of art and each model year was anxiously awaited. No one ever asked, "Where are the car keys?" because they were never taken out of the ignition. It was a time when music and cars were a way of life. There were no shopping malls. Fast food restaurants were just arriving. Drive-in restaurants had car hops and drug stores had soda jerks. Five & dime stores like F.W. Woolworth and S.H. Kress were a common sight.

During the 50's, there were numerous life-

changing events. From my perspective, perhaps four of these are in the top ten in changing the course of American life: Senator Albert Gore, Sr. spearheaded the Interstate Highway system which opened up travel like nothing else in US history. Kemmons and Dorothy Wilson built the first Holiday Inn on Summer Avenue in Memphis and a zillion others shortly thereafter which provided safe, clean, and predictable lodging for the middle class. Danny Thomas gave birth to St. Jude Children's Research Hospital which has been the flag ship for fighting childhood illnesses that were then called "incurable." And now (thank God and Danny Thomas) they are known as catastrophic but not incurable!

For good measure, I'll throw in one more plaudit. This one goes to Garnet and Frieda Carter who ushered in an altogether innovative concept in tourism marketing and opened the door for numerous others who followed their lead. Never heard of them? Bet you saw the barns– *See Rock City!* The success of this project was due in large part to the work of the most incomparable barn painter of all time, Clark Byers, who painted SEE ROCK CITY signs on literally hundreds of barn roofs all over the Southeastern United States.   Even though it didn't begin in the 50's, Rock City Gardens on Lookout Mountain, Tennessee, hit full stride during this era.

Since all four of these developments had Tennessee roots, we who claim the Volunteer State as our own have a right to swell up with pride.

The 50's was a time before the Beatles, tie dying, bell bottoms, Afros, the Age of Aquarius, the counter culture, and hippies. Elvis was the closest thing to a counter culture and beatniks were tame predecessors to the hippies.

The 50's preceded riots in the streets and the emergence of the drug scene. The only white stuff we sniffed up our noses was salt water to clear up sinus infections. Smoking pot meant something on the stove was too hot. Marijuana was something Puerto Ricans smoked on New York City's West Side and was called "Mary Jane." We knew about it from Reader's Digest (the student addition for English literature classes.) In those days, dropping acid could get you expelled from chemistry lab.

But smoking tobacco and drinking beer?! Now that was another story, especially in college. Male students considered beer drinking the way female students did smoking cigarettes– a required course! Many squeaky clean 18-year-olds strolled onto college campuses without so much as ever having swigged a slurp of Binaca to cover the smell of beer or tobacco on their breath. But, before freshman week was half over, they had used a church key on a Schlitz and fired up a Marlboro. As a result, today there's a passel of middle-aged folks with major respiratory problems (if they're still around.)

The 50's State of Mind was...

Long before... Pins were in noses, and rings were on toesies. Long before... Piercing of tongues, cheeks, and thingies by women and men and other known dingies.

The 50's era pre-dated the Vietnam war, that awful scar on American history; a debacle whose impact will take a hundred years to fully understand, and a thousand years to get over.

Question: Were the 50's a Place in Time or a State of Mind? Answer: Both. For sure, it was *a period of time*; more importantly, it was *a state of mind*.

The 50's was the place in time that followed the victory of WW II, when American industrialization and expertise was turned from war time efforts to civilian good fortune. Cars were back, industry was booming, homes were being built. Perhaps most important of all in creating the 50's state of mind, television entered our lives and changed the course of American culture forever.

In addition, when War II ended in 1945, thousands of jubilant, hero-like, yet lonely and love-starved GI's came home to the land of the free and home of the brave. Numerous children were immediately conceived and born in record numbers.

Wearing the blinders that all was right with the world, at home and abroad, the sunshine of prosperity was on the horizon and rising rapidly as the free enterprise system was given massive intravenous doses of ingenuity and productivity.   That's also when *America the Beautiful* became pregnant with the 50's.

As the nation recovered from a mind-set of war and focused on recovery from war-torn wounds, somewhere in the late 40's, the 50's were born and would have quite a long run. Quite a long run, indeed. Actually, about fifteen years! Yeah, I know the math doesn't quite work, but I never was very good with figures. Besides, this is my story and I'm sticking to it and I'm saying the 50's state of mind prevailed for about fifteen years.

The birth of the mind-set of the 50's was a process that took place gradually over a period of time. Like a pregnant woman who sometimes must go through many hours and sometimes days of hard labor and travail before giving birth, so it was with the birth of the mind set of the 50's. To pinpoint when it started is nebulous. Not so, concerning its death.

The 50's State of Mind died November 22, 1963, when the President of the United States, John Fitzgerald Kennedy, was assassinated in Dallas, Texas, apparently by a lone gunman, Lee Harvey Oswald.

It's my guess that the video footage of those few seconds of infamy has been shown on American television more than any other ten things combined. Enough so, there are few people, young or old, who do not have it forever indelibly etched in their conscious memory. (As you read this, were you seeing it in your mind's eye? I thought so.)

Where were you when the 50's died? From school age to old age, only a few people don't remember with minuscule details hearing the news of President Kennedy's death. Me, too.

Stationed at the Naval Air Station in Pensacola, Florida, I was an Aviation Officer Candidate in the United States Navy. While on my way to sick bay for some medication for a severe migraine headache, a cadet came running out of his barracks frantically yelling, "Kennedy's been shot! Kennedy's been shot!"

"No way, man," I berated, "Don't kid about something like that!"

"It's the God-fault truth— heard it in the barracks. We're in deep shit! I swear, we're in deep shit," he said, even more frantically as he ran away still yelling, "Kennedy's been shot. Kennedy's been shot."

From that point until I reached sick bay, I was in a fog and the next thing I remember was seeing and hearing Walter Cronkite announcing the President was dead. I didn't see a doctor and got no medication for my headache, but the pain in my head changed to anguish in my heart and anxiety in my soul.

In late afternoon on the base, I would meet Martha, my beautiful bride of six months. We would spend most of the evening huddled in our 2-door hardtop, '63 Bonneville Pontiac listening to the continuing news reports regarding the assassination. Feeling sad, mad, and scared, we held each other in cuddling comfort wondering what in God's name lay before the world, the country, and our young lives.

During that weekend, with the arrest of Lee Harvey Oswald and his death at the hand of Jack Ruby, I knew we were part of a participating audience watching the unfolding of a tragic drama on the worldwide stage. I had a strange sense that something ominous and unfathomable was occurring, that history was being written unlike anything in my lifetime. However, it would be many years later before I remotely understood the full magnitude of the assassination of President John F. Kennedy.

At this point in my life, now qualifying as a senior citizen, I believe that November 22, 1963, really was *The Day the Music Died, The End of the Innocence,* and *Bye, Bye, Miss American Pie.* That fateful day was in fact, *The Death of the 50's State of Mind.*

John Fitzgerald Kennedy

1917-1963

The Classes of the 90's and Beyond

For someone in mid-life or beyond, it is somewhat surprising and even shocking to realize that the majority of today's undergraduate college students were born after 1985. In their lifetime, there has been only one pope and they can only really remember two presidents– three at the most and two of them had the same last name. They were in elementary school during the Persian Gulf War. They don't remember the Reagan Era and don't know he was shot and wounded by John Hinckley. They were not exposed to Watergate and have never heard of "Senator Sam."

The youth of today have no experiential awareness of the racial bigotry and injustice of the 50's such as: On August 24th, 1955, two white men in Greenwood, Mississippi, Roy Bryant and J.W. Milam, kidnaped and brutally murdered a 14-year-old black kid named Emmett Till because he allegedly whistled at a white woman. On September 23rd, the jury acquitted them. On December 1st, Rosa Parks was arrested because she refused to move to the back of the bus in Montgomery, Alabama– thus began the Civil Rights Movement.   In 1957, the Southern Christian Leadership Conference was formed which pushed young Dr. Martin Luther King, Jr. to the national forefront. The young people of the 90's and beyond have no experiential awareness of the Civil Rights Movement, and thankfully, never saw two water fountains side by side, one marked WHITE, the other COLORED.

➤

The classes of the 90's and beyond know nothing of glass milk bottles with no safety caps that were not hermetically sealed because no one had ever tried to poison a perfect stranger. They know nothing of wooden Coke cases and soft drinks in glass bottles that had to be opened with a bottle opener. The inside of the bottle cap was lined with cork. They don't remember Grapettes, Sugar Babies, or some God-forsaken concoction known as ice milk. They never saw a Pop Cola which was the soft drink with a bottle cap that had a number under each cork liner. If your cap had the numbers 7 or 11, you won a free Pop Cola.

Kids today know nothing of refrigerators and deep freezers that had to be defrosted, ice that was frozen in metal trays, and homemade ice cream made in a hand cranked wooden churn. Hopefully none of today's youth ever smoked rabbit tobacco, corn silks, cedar bark, grapevine, or two for a nickel cigars and doubtfully ever mixed Hershey's chocolate and sugar to make it look like they were chewing tobacco or dipping snuff.

Kids today don't remember headlight dimmer switches on the floor board, ignition switches on the dashboard, heaters mounted on the inside of the firewall, or having to use hand signals for cars without turn signals.

Today's kids don't know about pea-shooters, cork popguns, 45 RPM records, blue flashbulbs, pant leg clips for bicycles without chain guards, or soldering irons you heat on a gas burner. Today's young women have no idea what it means to "get a Toni."

They've never seen a wringer washing machine, an outdoor clothes line, pants stretchers, nor starch that didn't come in an aerosol can. They never saw a box of laundry detergent with a free water glass, dish, or towel hidden inside the box. They assume you could always buy clothes that had permanent press. They've never seen an Air-wick in a bathroom. They think bottled water has been around forever, and not in their wildest dreams could they imagine drinking water drawn by bucket from a well.

They've never heard of Castor Oil, Hadacol, Syrup of Black Draught, or Cod Liver Oil. They never had a skinned knee treated with Mercurochrome or Merthiolate. They never had a warm flannel cloth covered with Vicks salve pinned to their pajama top to treat the croup. Thank God for that!

They have never feared a nuclear war with the Soviet Union, and never heard of the Civil Defense, air raid shelters, or the term "duck and cover." They are too young to remember the mass suicide in Jonestown and Tiananmen Square means nothing to them. Their lifetime has always included AIDS. They've never had a Polio shot, and likely do not know what it is.

The classes of the 90's and beyond know nothing of the long hard fight for women's liberation; that feminism and sexism are modern words; that during the 50's women lawyers, doctors, and politicians were nearly non-existent. They do not know of a time when a woman didn't have control of her own body, when abortions were illegal and performed only in back alleys, mostly by un-licensed physicians and nurses, and were often fatal.

Kids today have no idea what a pull-top can looks like. They know nothing of long playing vinyl record albums. Heck, they've never owned a record player. The expression "you sound like a broken record" means nothing to them. Very few of them have played *Pac Man*. The special effects in the original *Star Wars* and *Jaws* look pathetic to them. As far as they know, there have always been red M & M's, blue ones are not new, nor orange ones at Halloween.

Today's youth have never been to a sock hop; never heard of Sandra Dee, Troy Donahue, Fabian, the Mickey Mouse Club or Annette Funicello. Some of them read Jack Shaefer's *Shane* for English literature and may have seen "that old geeky movie" but they have no idea how much it touched a whole generation who heard little Joey Starritt cry out, "Shane, come back Shane. Shaaaaane."

James Dean, who starred in *East of Eden*, *Rebel Without a Cause*, and *Giant* overwhelmed our generation. Even though he died in a car wreck in 1955 at 24 years old, "James Dean" Leather jackets are still being sold today by the thousands.

In a very short 50's career, Hank Williams, Sr. changed country music forever. Songs he wrote and sang such as *Your Cheating Heart, I'm So Lonesome I Could Cry,* and *Cold Cold Heart* were the first country songs to crossover to the pop music charts. He died at age 29 from an overdose of pills and booze in the back seat of a white Cadillac in 1953.

Today's generation never used an 8-track tape, never saw the television phenomenon, *Laugh In,* and therefore have no idea what is meant by the phrase, "Sock it to me!" They don't remember the CB radio craze and would be dumbfounded to hear this transmission: "10-4, good buddy, you got a smokey at the 120 on yoh side. I be west bound with the hammer down headed to Mama in Shakey Town."

The Compact Disc was introduced before they were born. As far as they know, stamps have always cost about thirty something cents. They have always had an answering machine and have never seen a rotary dial telephone. Black and white televisions with only thirteen channels are unheard of to them. They have always had cable t.v and they could not fathom not having a remote control.

The classes of the 90's and beyond missed the life-changing influence of two of Dr. Martin Luther King's incredible speeches: "I Have a Dream" and "I've Seen the Promised Land." They've probably heard portions of these gems from television clips. However, to truly experience and appreciate the full level of inspirational, motivational, and spiritual intensity, you had to be there, living life in the chaos of the times. You really did.

As surprising as it is, Sony introduced the *Walkman* before they were born. Roller skating has always meant inline roller blades and they've never seen a skate key. *The Tonight Show* host has always

been Jay Leno. They have no idea when or why
Jordache jeans were cool and popcorn has always
been cooked in a microwave.

Since typewriters have long since been obsolete,
kids today never used carbon paper or correction fluid
and never had the pleasure of replacing a typewriter
ribbon. They've never used an ink blotter, fountain
pen, ink bottle with an ink well for filling the pen,
nor a fountain pen that used cartridges.

Miracle working, handheld calculators have always
been around which means they've never used an
adding machine and never heard of a slide rule.

Kids entering college today do not remember a
time when all gays, (men and women) were still "in
the closet." They do not know that forty years ago
the overwhelming majority of society held the
distorted view that homosexuals were sick, mentally
deranged, and therefore complete outcasts.

They never took a swim and thought about *Jaws*.
The Vietnam War is as ancient history to them as the
Civil War. They have no idea that Americans were
ever held hostage in Iran and they know nothing
about how President Jimmy Carter's diplomacy saved
those lives. They've probably heard of Jimmy and
Rosalyn Carter's march to the White House from
tiny, Plains, Georgia, but they never heard of brother,
Billy. Maybe that's just as well.

They can not fathom something called hard
contact lenses. They never heard the phrases:
"Where's the beef?" "I'd walk a mile for a Camel," or
"De plane, de plane!" To them, "It's cold enough to
kill hogs," has something to do with the
Tennessee/Arkansas football game.

They have no idea who J.R. is and could care even

less who shot him. To them Michael Jackson has always been nearly white. Until recent movies revived them, they thought *Charlie's Angels* had something to do with Della Reese and maybe was an episode of *Touched by an Angel.* They've always had MTV. They've seen more nudity in movies than most of us saw in the first ten years of marriage. They've never known a time when toothpaste, deodorant, razor blades and condoms weren't displayed side by side. Or as a Louisiana Cajun would say, "side by each."

Computers and email have always been available giving them vast exposure to the information age which is more mass knowledge than we had access to in our first thirty years. Maybe forty. Fifty?

But of all the items and inventions that changed their future adult lives, the number one thing that impacted them more than they'll ever know is Pampers!

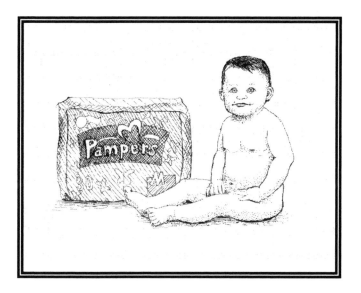

I truly believe the invention of disposable diapers is in the top five of all the important inventions in the history of humankind. Right up there with fire, the wheel, the safety pin, and dental floss. I'm also sure there's no way for the younger generation to even remotely comprehend what I'm talking about. But as feeble as this explanation will be, let me try to explain with just a short version of this process.

First, you remove the baby's flannel pajama bottoms that were wet because the rubber pants had leaked. Then you remove and wash out a cloth nighttime diaper filled with three pounds of urine, or that other bodily function that would gag a maggot. Now you wash out the disgusting dirty diaper in the toilet and wring the water out of it, and deposit it in a   diaper pail that is already loaded with a dozen others... young people, trust me on this one– unless you've been there, you cannot comprehend it. Yeah, to understand it, you definitely have to have been there and done that.

This disposable diaper story is a humorous microcosm of what I'm trying to say about the big picture of my generation. The youth of the 90's and beyond can not possibly image what life was like for the youth of the 50's. But we know, still remember, and hopefully will never forget.

Parsons, Tennessee

Home of 2452 Friendly Folks and 8-10 Old Grouches
(A Genuine Small Town)

Well I was born in a small town
And I live in a small town
Prob'ly die in a small town
Oh, those small communities

Educated in a small town
Taught the fear of Jesus in a small town
Used to daydream in that small town
Another boring romantic that's me

No I can't forget where I come from
I cannot forget the people who love me
Yeah, I can be myself in this small town
And people let me be what I want to be

John Cougar Mellencamp

What qualifies as a *small town?* How about this–
*A small town is where people know when you're born and
care when you die.* I think that's what John Cougar
Mellencamp was saying in his hit song. If there's any
truth in that statement, then Parsons, Tennessee,
was, is, and always will be "a small town." The people
who grew up there and those who continue to live
there are mighty proud of it– myself included. I've
been gone from that small town for more than forty
five years, but it's still an integral part of my life. Due
to the influences that helped shape me and the
memories that continue to guide me, the people of
Parsons and the class of '59 are the realities of my
youth and my reference point for life in the 50's. To
each and every one in that small town, I salute you.

➤

During our high school years, Dwight Eisenhower
and Richard Nixon were our leaders. The country
was terrified of communism. The cold war was very
cold. Senator Joe McCarthy made a career out of the
terror of communism, blacklisting, and witch hunting
for anyone who might be communist sympathizers.
The most powerful Tennessee politicians were Estes
Kefauver, Frank Clement, and Albert Gore, Sr. "The
Senator" as he was known.

Patriotism was big in the 50's– at least, that's what
we called it. In actuality, it just meant waving the
flag, singing *The National Anthem* with velocity and
enthusiasm, and of course, getting misty eyed when
Kate Smith sang, "God Bless America."

Speaking of patriotism, it reached an intense level
when the Russians sent their space capsule, Sputnik,
orbiting the earth. In fact, that patriotism was
accompanied with an enormous amount of fear which

propelled Congress to push NASA to catch and pass the Soviet Union in the race to outer space. And they did. Alan Shepard was the first to strap himself inside a Mercury project capsule, followed by Gus Grissom, and then John Glenn took the first ride that actually orbited the good earth.

In addition to exploration of the heavens, we were also making great strides probing the depth of the deep blue seas. In 1955, the first nuclear powered submarine made her maiden voyage. Three years later, *Nautilus* departed Pearl Harbor on a mission to accomplish the first ship's crossing of the North Pole. "For the World, Our Country, and the Navy– the North Pole" declared Commander William Anderson, of Waverly, Tennessee. With a crew of 116 men aboard, under Commander Anderson's watchful eye, *Nautilus* had accomplished the "impossible," sailing under the icecap of the North Pole. What a victory.

However, eight years later on April 10, 1963, another nuclear powered sub met horrible disaster as the USS Thresher sank 220 miles east of Boston while conducting deep-diving exercises. All aboard– 16 officers, 96 enlisted men and 17 civilians– died in that tragedy.

Summertime in the 50's was a time of fear and anxiety for parents because children by the thousands became infected with the crippling disease, poliomyelitis. This burden of fear was lifted forever when it was announced on April 12, 1955, that Dr. Jonas Salk had developed a vaccine against polio– one of the greatest medical breakthroughs of all time.

In the 50's, we had baseball, real baseball (that really sounds like an old foggie. Right?!) Stan "The

Man" Musial and Enos "Country" Slaughter were stars for the Cardinals. Duke Snider and Roy Campanella were Dodgers, who were still in Brooklyn. There were no Atlanta Braves.

Lauren Bacall and Katherine Hepburn were Hollywood starlets along with newcomers Elizabeth Taylor and Marilyn Monroe.   Clark Gable and Spencer Tracy were still idolized. Randolph Scott was a western star. John Wayne was in all the war movies, although he never served in the military. There was still a debate about who was really the king of the cowboys, Roy Rogers or Gene Autry.   Charlton Heston played MOSES, and in his later years seemed to believe that he really was.

In the 50's, automobile radios were AM only; it was called a Deluxe model if it had push buttons; there was only one speaker per radio. Stereo was just coming around to replace Hi-Fi. As we became familiar with stereo, a lot of jokes emerged. "Did you hear they're now making stereo deodorant?" "Really?" "Yeah– it doesn't make you smell any better but you can't tell which armpit it's coming from!" That could be followed by a "Little Moron" joke or a "Knock Knock" joke. (We weren't the inventors of corny jokes but we did spread them around.)

In that era, there was no such thing as icemakers, microwaves, dishwashers, garbage disposals and compactors, (that ingenious device that turns twenty pounds of garbage into, well, twenty pounds of garbage.) Few of our homes were air conditioned and most of those were window units only. Most of the homes were cooled with window fans that ran from May to October day and night. There was no such thing as coffee makers. Coffee was made in percolators that lasted a life time. Martha and I still have one that was given to us as a wedding present in 1963– a General Electric model that works as well today as it did brand new.

Early in our youth, we played *Hide and Go Seek, Simon Says, Red Light/Green Light, Hopscotch, Annie Over, Kickball, Dodgeball, and Mother May I.* We wore wax lips and mustaches, drank Big Oranges, RC Colas, and NEHIS. We ate Moon Pies, Armstrong's Fried Pies, and Mrs. Sullivan's Pecan Pies. (Seems like we were really into pies in those days.) Boys aggravated the girls with pea shooters, water pistols, spit balls, and shot at each other with BB guns when our mothers didn't know it. We ravaged June apple trees and grape vines from neighbors orchards and ate huckleberries when we were in the woods.

We ran through the water hose sprinkler, made slingshots and bows and arrows from hickory limbs. We rolled each other downhill inside old car tires. Sometimes our mothers even made outdoor flower pots out of those old tires. We went barefoot a lot and knocked the skin off our toes trying to learn to ride bicycles on gravel roads. On lazy spring and summer afternoons, we flew homemade and store bought kites over big sage-grass fields.

At night, we played *Kick the Can*, caught lightning

bugs (fire flies to city folks) in Mason jars, laid on the grass looking for a shooting star, and tried to figure what a certain collection of stars reminded us of. "See those right there! Looks just like grandpa's hat!" "You crazy, man. You making that up. You don't see nothing!" "Do too." "Do not." "Do too!"

When city kids came to visit in the summer, we took them on snipe hunts. That's the one where a kid would be left in the woods to hold the sack for a snipe while the others when off to flush it out. Then everyone would sneak off and leave the kid "holding the bag."

On Sunday afternoons, we sometimes played "pocketbook." We'd get an old purse (which country folks called a pocketbook), tie a long piece of fishing line to it, lay it in the middle of a highway and hide in the bushes. When someone spotted the purse, stopped their car and got out to pick it up, we'd jerk the string and they'd know "they'd been had."

In the early 50's, television was still in its infancy; radio was still the king of entertainment. We listened intently to *Fibber McGee & Molly, Amos & Andy, Burns & Allen, Arthur Godfrey, Bob & Ray, Stella Dallas, Charlie McCarthy, Don McNeill's Breakfast Club*, and who could ever forget *The Inner Sanctum* with that awesomely, scarey "creaking door."

Most of us cut our own Christmas trees out in the woods. Normally cedar. Bubble lights and angel hair were the new inventions for decorating the tree. We thought they were fantastic.

Our dogs were mostly strays, mixed breeds sometimes called "Heinz 57's" or "mongrels." They ran loose. Hugh and Lorraine Houston raised Pomeranians which was the only purebreds most of us had ever seen. In Bell's Grocery, a kid named Chris Dawes asked Mr. Hugh how much he got for his puppies. Holding one in his arm, Hugh replied, "A woman offered me $75 for this one, but I turned it down." Chris replied, "Mr. Hugh, if that had been me, the lady would've owned a new dog!" (To put it in perspective, minimum wage was $.90 per hour.)

During the 50's , seamless nylons were introduced and then spandex was added making them stretchy This God-send eliminated baggy stockings forever. Then came pantyhose which "reshaped" American women and greatly altered spontaneous sex forever after. Bonnet style hair dryers came along in the 50's. So did aerosol cans and Sweet & Lo.

In 1958, masses of people went "crazy as hoot owls" over one of the most phenomenal fads in human history– the Hoola Hoop. Okay, okay, I had one, too. Didn't you? We used LifeBuoy ("It Floats") and Lava soap and collected S&H Green stamps. 3-D movies were introduced and *The House of Wax* scared us spitless. On weekends, we often went to the "passion pit" known to our parents as the Drive-In.

Even though we didn't know it, we were already environmentally correct because   all soft drink bottles were used over and over again– we were into recycling without being cognizant of it.

Guys turned their jeans up and used a little dab of Bream cream; girls turned their socks down and wore poodle skirts and pony tails. We used terms like "smooching" and "making out." Some guys and girls were "going steady" and to show it, he would give her his class ring and she would wrap the inside with adhesive tape, or melt candle wax inside so it would fit her finger. Or, she'd wear his ring around her neck while singing the chorus from that great song by Elvis– *Won't you wear my ring around your neck, to show the world, I'm yours by heck!* Powerful lyrics– powerful!!

College girls got "dropped" which should not be confused with breaking up or getting laid. The more astute called it "lavoliered." Either way, it meant if a guy and girl were getting pretty serious about their relationship, he would give her a necklace with his fraternity letters on it– thus lavoliered or dropped. If they were really getting tight, she got pinned which should not be confused with any activity that might have taken place in the back seat of the '57 Chevy. No, getting pinned meant he gave her his fraternity pin which was essentially the last step before getting officially engaged with a ring– lots of touchy feely, huggy kissy, and all that stuff.

Speaking of kissing or slapping, as the case might be; at night, when a car load of guys and gals were just out driving and you saw an oncoming vehicle with only one headlight, if the guy yelled "Cockeye, popeye, pe-didle" before the girl did, he got to kiss her. If she yelled those sophisticated words first, she got to slap him! Go figure. I was usually a little slow on the trigger in playing this game. Maybe that's why I've always had red cheeks... .

Radio stations (they were A.M. only) blasted out music by Elvis, the Coasters, Little Richard, the Platters, Bill Haley and the Comets, Johnny Cash, and Patsy Cline (who was only 30 when she died in an airplane crash.) We listened to a lot of that music while "going parking" "making out" trying to learn *brail anatomy* at the river, or on water tank hill.

The 50's were filled with music and television capitalized on it. We were fascinated by the novel idea of following the bouncing ball in *Sing Along With Mitch*. When we thought we wouldn't get caught, we watched a little of Lawrence Welk just to hear Pete Fountain, Big Tiny Little, Joanne Castle, the Lennon Sisters, and to hear the Maestro say, "Thank you boys, and thank you Bobby & Sissy."

We watched *The Honeymooners* with Jackie Gleason,

Art Carney, and Audrey Meadows. We loved the bit where Frank Fontaine did his punch-drunk character, Crazy Guggenheim. After some comedic dialogue with the Mr. Donahue, the bartender,(Jackie)old Frank would sing with a smooth as honey baritone that would make a grown man cry. But the big deal of the times was the birth of Rock & Roll, Doo Wop, and Rockabilly and we listened to it all and liked it all. Whether parking or driving, we tuned in Randy's and Ernie's out of Nashville and Dewey Phillips's Red, Hot, and Blue out of Memphis. And just for fun, sometimes on a Saturday night, we would tune in to XERA from Del Rio, Texas, where they sold on the air, chenille bed spreads with the 23rd Psalm on them and commode top covers with the Lord's Prayer.

Sam Phillips founded Sun Records in 1952 and in a stroke of luck and genius, in the next few years, signed and recorded– Elvis Presley, Jerry Lee Lewis, Johnny Cash, Carl Perkins, Bill Justice, Roy Orbison, Conway Twitty and Charlie Rich. Wow!

What I'm trying to say is, during this era music came alive! It was new, enriching, and saturated with inspiring lyrics and uplifting titles. Titles that would challenge the mind, tug at the heart, and stir the soul. I'm talking heavy stuff. Titles like: "Tootie Fruity" and "Nel Blu di Pinto di Blu." A group called the Champs sang "Tequila." I doubt that many of us even knew what it was, but we learned. Sheb Wooley wrote and sang "The Flying Purple People Eater." And there was "Bird Dog" "Yakety Yak" "Poison Ivy"

"Bony Moronie" "Good Golly, Miss Molly" "Long Tall Sally" and, if you can believe this, Connie Francis sang one called "Stupid Cupid." And who could ever forget that once in a lifetime classic by the Chordettes (sung better by our classmates Diane Tinker and Sara Don Gibson) called "Lollipop."

Along with the music craze, dancing was hot and a bevy of dance steps and styles were introduced and tried: jitterbug, cha cha, bop, stroll, twist, and the watusee. We watched the kids dance on Dick Clark's American Bandstand and tried to do what they did. We loved the music and especially the great lyrics. Are you ready for this?!

"Oh little darlin, I was wronga, to thinka, that I coulda lovea twoa, oh whoa, oh wella, ..."

***

"A wanga dang dang, a wanga dang, Blue Moon..."

***

"Yakety yak, yakety yak, don't talk back..."

Man, if that stuff wouldn't ring your fast-dancing bell, your clapper must be broke!

Then for a little slow dancing, we'd get cheek to cheek and sometimes the girl would put both hands behind her back and the guy would have his arms around her holding her hands, and it would be, well, uh, er, real close. Singing off key in each other's ears:

"My love, my darling, I hunger for your touch..."
"This is dedicated to the one I love..."
"You are my special angel..."

Believe me, that kind of music would intensify the urge to merge!

Channel 7 in Jackson had a program called "Teen Time Dance Party." Each Saturday morning the show featured a different high school from around the region with 10-12 couples competing. PHS had its turn, and I, along with several others, paired up and starting practicing for our big television debut.

Our dancing stars (who really could cut a rug) were brother and sister combo, Jimmy Joe and Janie Readey. Man, were they good! Running a close second was Philip Brasher and Ann Jordan. In my case, when it came to dancing, I was more than a little bit gauche but I was smart enough to hook up with Suzanne Hartsfield as my partner. Suzanne was a stunningly beautiful girl who "could really work a room." So **my** dancing really didn't matter, nobody was looking at me anyway! **She** took third place, I smiled a lot and accepted my ribbon.

Toward the end of the 50's and early 60's a new music style emerged that would take the country by storm. Originating on the West Coast, Folk Music really caught on with the college crowd– Judy Collins, Pete Seeger, Smothers Brothers, Kingston Trio, Brothers Four, Limelighters, Joan Baez, Peter Paul and Mary, Highwaymen, New Christie Minstrels, Glenn Yarbrough– and many more sang music that captured the heart and soul of American youth. Sung in coffee houses, on college campuses, and clubs like the Hungry I and Purple Onion in San Francisco, folk music was incredibly popular.

A Saturday night television program called

Hootenanny was a major contributor to the folk music craze and was the showcase for many of those who became standards in the field. It was great music for live performances because so much of it was sing-along type and the audiences were a vital part of the process– *There's a Meeting Here Tonight, Tom Dooley, This Land is Your Land, Greenfields, Michael Row the Boat Ashore, Midnight Special, Big Rock Candy Mountain, Cottonfields, Rock Island Line* – these tunes just seemed to require audience participation.

Some of it was lighthearted and shallow but some was heavy and quite political and helped raise the consciousness of America's youth regarding social issues and human rights. During the 60's, folk music would reach even greater heights and have a more profound impact but the origin of this musical phenomenon was squarely in the 50's.

➤

Before going further, let's do a reality check to see if you're a bonafide member of the 50's or just a closet wannabe. Believe me, that's a serious problem! Today, there are many young adult 50's wannabees who are masquerading as products of that era. But, we who are authentic 50's old timers are doing our best to weed them out before this problem becomes somber.

So, here's the deal– take the following test and then we'll know if you're the real deal or just a hopeless wannabe. OR, perhaps you're really from the 50's and just having a senior citizen moment, sometimes known as CRS– Can't Remember_ _ _ _!

50'S QUIZ

Fill in the blanks *before* looking at the answers below.

QUESTIONS:

1. "You'll wonder where the yellow went _____."
2. Muhammad Ali's original name was _____.
3. "M-i-c-k-e-y _____."
4. "Hey kids, what time is it?" "_____."
5. "Oh, I wonder, wonder, who; _____?"
6. "He was kinda' broad at the shoulder, and narrow at the hip, everybody knew you didn't give no lip to_____."
7. "I found my thrill _____."
8. "As I walk through my Dukedom, nothing can stop the _____."
9. "Good night, Mrs. Calabash, _____."
10. "Good night, David." "Good night,_____."

ANSWERS:

1. "When you brush your teeth with Pepsodent."
2. Cassius Clay
3. "M-o-u-s-e."
4. "It's Howdy Dowdy time."
5. "Who wrote the book of love."
6. "Big John."
7. "On Blueberry Hill."
8. "Duke of Earle."
9. "Wherever you are." (Spoken by Jimmy Durante.)
10. "Good night, Chet." (David Brinkely and Chet Huntley– NBC news anchors.)

All bonafide old 50's folks will score at least 70%. If you got less than 5 correct you're definitely a 50's wanna be or you're already experiencing half-heimers (the condition that precedes Alzheimer's.)

The Tennessee River

Alvin C. York Bridge, Decatur County, TN

*"Oh, the Tennessee River and a mountain man, we'll
get together every time we can."*

Since we didn't have any mountains in Decatur
County, those words by the singing group *Alabama*
may not have been a total fit. But I do know one
thing– we were living in California when the song
came out, and every time I heard it, I got a lump in
my throat and felt a little homesick. The reason
being– it brought back numerous memories of the
Alvin C. York Bridge, Perryville, the Beech River
Bridge, and the Tennessee River.

When I was in elementary school one of my
family's summer time rituals was a week of trotline
fishing. My father (Maxie Doyle) along with Uncle
George (George Harrell) and Uncle Harrell (Harrell
Watson) always took their vacations at the same time

so they could fish. Some of the time I was allowed to go along on these outings. What a treat! Numerous stories could be told from those experiences but for sure, one must be included.

One of the fish that was caught in the Tennessee River was called a "spoon bill catfish." It was weird looking with a head that had a long flat bill protruding like an extended nose. They were not considered edible which is where this story begins.

One morning as my father and two uncles were leaving their boat after having finished running their trotlines, a man stopped them to show them his "catch." It was a very large spoon bill catfish and he was extremely proud. It was obvious that he didn't know very much about fishing, "Probably a city slicker from up North," surmised my father.

Uncle George said, "Fella, that's some mighty good eating if you cook him right."

"Oh yeah? How's that?"

"Well, you build a big fire and then let it burn down to get some good hot coals. While the fire's burning down, you clean your fish good. Just open him up and gut him and then get a wooden board about two feet long. Tack that fish to the board and when the coals are just right, you hold him over those coals for about 30 minutes, cooking it real slow. Then when it's a nice golden brown, you throw that fish into the fire and eat the board!"

After they stopped laughing and the forlorn stranger turned to walk away, Uncle George gave him two fine fiddler catfish out of their morning catch.

Growing up in Parsons in the 50's meant going to the river a lot– sometimes to ski, sometimes not. Some people fished the river for fun or a living; others were involved in the mussel business.

Fresh water mussels are basically the equivalent of salt water clams and their shells were used for making buttons, mostly in Japan. To gather mussels, a man would stay out on the river all day, drop down brails on mussel beds and then hoist up the catch. I did that one summer. Didn't make much money, but met a lot of interesting people and picked up some good education about life, including men and women, husbands and wives. Earl Pratt was my mussleing mentor, and "Tight Eye" Tyler, the man I worked for, was everybody's mentor about life and living. I didn't believe a whole lot of what he said about life, living, and the pursuit of happiness but I did appreciate his fairness and his acceptance of me as a total outsider whom he respected and appreciated. I can still remember some of his philosophizing about the problems between men and women, husbands and wives and how he tied it in with the Genesis passages concerning Adam and Eve in the Garden of Eden.

Just thinking about that brings a smile to my face. I can still see the seriousness and intensity on Tight Eye's face (mostly his good eye) sitting on that stump giving us young guys the inside scoop about when the problems started between male and female. In fact, I'd give a $100 to have it on tape.

During my musseling days, I also got to know a man known as "Old Timer," a commercial fisherman who was wise, gentle, and helpful. He wore a big black western style hat with a feather in it and it was rumored that he was "part Cherokee Indian."

One morning as I was loading my boat to catch the "current" for some early musseling, Old Timer was coming in after being out early catching bait for his trot lines. His boat was next to mine. He looked over at me and said, "Look what tried to get in the boat with me." Looking around, I saw him holding up a six-foot rattlesnake. "Wow." I roared. Almost apologetic, Old Timer said, "I tried to shoo him off but he was kinda sassy and kept on acting hateful, so I busted him with the boat paddle."

Much earlier, I had figured out that if a fight ever broke out down at the river, I was going to be on Old Timer's side. After that morning, I was sure of it.

Speaking of snake stories. Bobby Myracle and I nearly lost a couple of girls one Saturday afternoon over a snake. The four of us were at the river for some skiing and fun and I was pulling the boat into the bank. Bobby was in the front and reached up to catch a limb from a small tree to cushion the impact against the rocky shore.

Lying out on that limb was a green snake about eighteen inches long taking a nice snooze in the sun. Bobby never saw it. I did. Just as I was about to warn him, he turned the limb loose and it sprang back to its normal position. You guessed it. In slingshot fashion, that green snake shot off the limb and landed right in the middle of us. Both girls screamed and went up on each side of the boat. I thought they were going over and the water was quite deep in that area. But with calm, cool, forced macho and moxie, I snatched the snake up by the tail and tossed it in the water. Did it scare me? Nah. Couldn't look bad in front of those girls. However, I admit that my already wet bathing suit gave me a little extra protection from any possible embarrassing sight!

Now that I'm on a roll, how about some more snake stories?! During the summer I mowed lawns which sometimes included yards that were overgrown or vacant lots that had never been cut with a lawn mower. One of my regular customers was "Miss Bill" Barnett and on one occasion she wanted me to cut the deepest part of her back lot that was long overdue. The first time around I cut it with the blade very high and then lowered it for a second cutting.

During the second round, Miss Bill came out to watch and, of course, to supervise. As I turned a corner very near where she was standing, a copperhead snake came tearing out of the grass headed downhill to get away from my lawn mower that was obviously bearing down on his cozy little nest. She threw her hands up and screamed bloody murder, "Get him, get him, get him!" Of course, I would have done it anyway, but with her blood curdling insistence, I kicked into high gear and started after the snake– with the lawn mower you understand! Running over him I stopped to let the mower take care of business, but to my surprise that snake came out the front of the mower and he, too, was now in high gear. I stayed after him but every time I ran over him and stopped, he'd come out the other end without a scratch. The grass was so high and thick that snake was able to stay low enough to avoid the blade from my mower. After four or five of these near misses, we came to a little rise in the yard that didn't have as much grass and that's when the copperhead met his waterloo. By then, Miss Bill was on the back porch fanning herself trying to ward off the vapors and I was an eleven-year-old boy smiling from ear to ear at having sent a deadly poisonous pit viper to the promised land. When Miss Bill paid me, she added an extra quarter for the snake.

Several years later, I would have the Bejesus scared out of me in what is yet another snake story. We were water skiing one Sunday afternoon and one of the bindings on my slalom came loose. So, we pulled the boat– a 15 foot Feathercraft– into the bank near the Striegel Brothers Beech River Boat Dock to fix the ski. With the ski laying across the back of the boat, I was repairing it while standing in waist deep river. And to my total surprise and shock, a cottonmouth water moccasin poked his head out of the water between me and the boat! In a nano-second and with one giant leap, I landed in the boat shaking like a leaf. My ski pals laughed their heads off– I didn't think it was very funny myself!

That'll do it for the snake stories but the aforementioned does bring up a couple of great memories about water skiing which, except for team sports, was my greatest recreational passion. We had a homemade ski jump that was great fun but caused a lot of bumps and bruises on many a wanna be macho young man. We tried our hand at emulating the Cypress Gardens ski show by having girls riding on the backs and necks of guys, double, triple and quadruple skiing and making pyramids. We weren't very good, but it was great fun.

To top it off, I had the infamous distinction (as far as anybody knew) of being the only person to ever get caught in a trotline while water skiing. It was not a source of pride but was the topic of much conversation and it left some indelible reminders of that inauspicious occasion on both legs in the form of permanent scars. It's really too long and too complicated a story to tell so I think I'll just leave it at that. Besides, your imagination has probably made it much worse than it really was!

At night, we often went to the river to watch "submarine races." For those who need a translation, that meant boys and girls doing a lot of talking, teasing, and smooching. In the summertime, watching submarine races in cars without air conditioning could get to be a heated situation. In the wintertime, even with the car running and the heater on, it meant seeing a car with fogged windows, which also could get to be a rather heated situation.

Movies & Miscellaneous

We went to the movies a lot. All theaters had ushers with flashlights who escorted you to your seat and would frequently come down the aisle and call someone's name to report to the lobby– "Bill Snodgrass, you're wanted up front." We thought the *Rustic Theater* was great and grieved when Hobart Goff replaced it with a grocery store. Then we were left with *The Times* in Decaturville or we could go to Lexington to the *Princess* or the *Strand*. In those days, we didn't go to the movies, we went to "the show" where we saw Serials, News Clips about world events, and usually a Comedy, such as: *Heckel and Jeckel, The Bowery Boys, Tom and Jerry, Mr. Magoo, Our Gang,* and last but not least, *Woody Woodpecker*. Man, were we classy, or what?! And finally, the Main Feature.

On Saturday afternoons you could go to the show for a dime where you'd see a comedy, news clips from world events, a serial, and the feature which was always a western. The Saturday matinee and evening serials included such things as *Tarzan,* played by Johnny Weismueller, *Ramah of the Jungle, Rocket Man, Flash Gordon,* and *Jungle Jim*.

The cowboy stars were: Johnny Mack Brown, Sunset Carson, Lash LaRue, Rocky Lane, Red Ryder, Whip Wilson, Wild Bill Hickok, The Cisco Kid, Jimmy Wakeley, and Bob Steele.

Clayton Moore was the Lone Ranger, Bill Boyd was Hopalong Cassidy. Roy, Dale and Gene were Roy, Dale, and Gene. And who could forget the sidekick stars: George (Gabby) Hays, "Howdy,

Buckaroos!"; Pancho,"Oh Cisco!"; Jay Silverheels was a great Tonto, "Me not know, Kemosabie"; Andy Devine was Jingles, "Hey, Wild Bill, wait for me!" Slim Pickens was in dozens of movies, Robert Blake was "Little Beaver"and Dub Taylor was "Cannonball."

We were fascinated with animal stars in the movies and on television. Trigger, Champ, Rin Tin Tin, Fury, Cheetah, My Friend Flicka, Lassie, and King– as Sergeant Preston would say, "On King, on you huskies."

In the theaters, at intermission, just before the main feature, you could run out to the lobby and get a five cent bag of popcorn with real butter from Jack Goff, the concessionaire. Donald "Popcorn" Moore was Jack's main man and I filled in on occasion for Donald. If your appetite was heavy, your money in good shape, and you didn't have a date, you'd go for a BOX of popcorn– a real box of popcorn with real butter. To make sure folks got their money's worth, we'd push the narrow ends toward the middle so the sides would push out, then we turned the top flaps up to form barriers so the box would hold more corn. When patrons weren't looking, we'd add a dash of salt to the box which would make them come back for more and of course another drink at the fountain. A box like that cost a dime and a delicious cherry coke float was a ten cent item, also.

One Saturday night when Donald Moore was away and I had the popcorn machine by myself was indeed a memorable experience. A fellow named Alton Rossen, who was well known for his voracious appetite for popcorn, came up and ordered two boxes for himself. I added the real butter and a little extra salt. By intermission, he was the first in line and this time, he ordered two sacks. Buttering it up good, I added the little extra salt. You guessed it– he was back before the feature ended to get another sack of popcorn. By my count, he had eaten two boxes and three sacks of pop corn which was the equivalent of at least one and a half gallons. And he drank three large Dixie Cups of fountain coke. Glad I didn't have to sleep in the same room with my friend, Alton Rossen, that night!

We hung out at the Dairy Bar and Faye Inman's Snack Bar where Gladys Herndon made the best hamburger in the world for twenty cents. With lettuce, tomato, and cheese it was twenty five. It cost a nickel to play the Wurlitzer jukebox, or you could play six for a quarter– if you had one. Much of the time, we just stood around or sat around and "watched traffic." Sometimes late on a weekend night, I'd spot Robert Fisher in the Snack Bar and I'd make a beeline for his table. He was in college and later medical school and I was eager to listen to his latest stories. I also soaked up his encouragement to pursue higher education. Robert was a few years older than me but he always seemed to value my company. In turn, I'll be forever grateful for his positive influence on my life while sitting in Faye Inman's Snack Bar, talking, drinking coffee or coke, and "watching traffic."

In the 50's, Coca Cola bottles had the city where it was bottled printed on the bottom. Guys often played "far away" to see whose came from the longest distance. "Whatcha got?" "Atlanta." "Beatcha, I got Denver!" "You lie!" "Oh, yeah? Look!" "Dang!" In the late 50's, soft drinks went up to six cents. In vending machines the extra penny was on the honor system. You put a nickel in the machine and a penny in the coin box attached to the side.

Gasoline came in two flavors only– Regular at thirty cents a gallon (twenty-nine at Bill Perry's) and High Test which was thirty two. Few of us ever bought more than a dollar's worth at the time. But even if you bought only a buck worth of gas, the attendant still checked your oil and water, cleaned your windshield, front and back, and if they needed it, put air in your tires. My! My! Isn't self-service wonderful?!

Speaking of service stations and such reminds me of how many of us were already driving before we got our driver's license. As long as we stayed out of the main part of town, it was somewhat understood that 14 and 15 year old kids could drive without being harassed by the city police. I was delivering newspapers in my own car– a '52 Willis sedan– long before I was 16 and had a license– which brings up another memory.

Parsons had access to five daily newspapers! Both Nashville papers– *The Tennessean* and *Nashville Banner*; both Memphis papers– *The Commercial Appeal* and *Memphis Press Scimitar*, and *The Jackson Sun*. Numerous teenage boys made their spending money from throwing papers– myself included. Dale Roberts, along with twin brothers, Bill and Bob had a lock on the Nashville papers for years. For a time, I carried both Memphis papers with help from my brother, Mickey. Some of the fondest memories of my youth involved the newspaper business.

On one occasion, I was out trying to get new customers for my paper route and making a big sales pitch to Berthal Haggard. Berthal subscribed to *The Jackson Sun* and I was trying to lure him away by giving him the advantages of my papers over the inferior *Sun*. When I finished, he said, "Son, I know you're right, either one of your papers has much more to offer than what I'm taking. And if I was reading your papers, I'd get a lot more news and stuff. But here's the deal. When I come home from work, I'm tired and just need to rest a little and I can read every word in *The Jackson Sun* and go to bed with nothing on my mind!" He laughed, patted me on the back, and said, "Keep up the good work." Having no retort to that argument, I laughed and thanked him and went on to the next prospective customer.

My afternoon paper, *The Memphis Press Scimitar*, was dropped off at Clebe Yates Esso Station. As soon as I could get there after school and sports practice, I'd head to the station to roll the papers and get ready to run my route. Clebe was my great uncle and one of my childhood heroes. By the time I got to his station, numerous times, he would have already rolled my papers for me. Can you believe that kind of support– which brings up a story that confirms why Clebe Yates was one of my childhood heroes.

During my second year of college, on a Sunday afternoon as I was headed back to school, I pulled into his Esso station for some gas. Trotting out to service my car, Clebe said, "When I saw you pull in, I said, here comes our town's next millionaire!" While he was dead wrong about that assessment, the value of such encouragement was immeasurable.

Back to the paper route business. Occasionally, other workers at the station such as Red Rogers or Jessie Douglas pitched in to help with the paper rolling chore. In addition, half a dozen friends would periodically gather to help roll papers and ride the route with me and we'd play "paper route basketball." Many years later, I was accused of using or manipulating them to do my work by preying on their fascination with playing ball. Now, I'm not saying I did, and I'm not saying I didn't, but I do know it helped me out a lot. My brother, Mickey, who was four years younger, was responsible for riding his bike and delivering the papers to our customers in the business district. I paid him a little but not a lot– sorry about that Bocephus.

Here's the scoop on "paper route basketball." As the driver, I was always one of the players who was being challenged by whomever got the "shotgun seat." The goal was simple– we threw the papers from inside the car while it was rolling and if the paper stayed on the porch, you got two points; if you missed the porch but it stayed on the sidewalk, you got one point. With maybe a coke at stake, by the end of the route the winner would be declared. Houston Barrett, Bob Herndon, Reed Patterson, Jay Wallace, Gary Carrington, Harry (Hoot) Turpin, Billy Tuten, and Larry Hayes were the main players, with others occasionally subbing. Guys were the afternoon riders but my morning route with *The Commercial Appeal* would usually include a girl or two. We didn't play "paper route basketball"– just mostly talked.

Throwing papers was a great learning experience and taught me a lot about managing money, dealing with people, and having to be accountable for my mistakes. A lot of my throws landed on rooftops and I must have broken out a dozen small glass pane basement windows in the Tim Boaz house. Even though I offered, he never let me pay for them. In fact, one time when I mentioned it, he told me that he kept an ample supply of replacements (that he brought from his hardware store) just to have them handy after I knocked out a glass.

Pat Long wasn't as benevolent and I paid the price (rightfully so) for one mishap with her paper. "Miss" Pat had a nice size front porch which was on my side of the car and was almost always a sure "two points" in paper route basketball. She also had a very large glass storm door. You're already way ahead of me, aren't you?!

One afternoon I was a little too strong on my shot and the paper hit square in the middle of the glass door. To add insult to injury, the wooden door was open. You guessed it– the paper broke the glass door into a thousand pieces and wound up under the sofa in her living room!   With fear and trembling, I went up to the door and rang the bell. She didn't answer so I called out to her through the giant hole in the front door. She still didn't answer. Somewhat relieved that she wasn't home, I left her a note telling her I was the culprit and would be back to settle up with her later in the afternoon. When I finished the route that day, I went back to "Miss" Pat's. She was home. When I explained what had happened, I concluded by saying, "You have it repaired and, of course, I'll pay for every penny of it." She wasn't as furious as I had expected but she did have an edge in her voice when she replied, "No, I won't have it repaired. You'll go to the hardware store and get the glass and come back and repair it yourself– here's a tape measure!"

"Yes Mam," is all I remember saying before measuring the opening and then going to Tim Boaz Hardware where Mr. Carl Partin cut the glass for me. After installing it in the front storm door, I cleaned up the glass on the front porch and in the living room, retrieved that edition of the *Press Scimitar* from under the sofa, and hand-delivered it to "Miss" Pat in her rocker where smilingly she began reading the afternoon news.

➤

Downtown Parsons

My Town
Where I was born, where I was raised.
Where I keep all my yesterdays.
Where I ran off 'cos I got mad,
And I came to blows with my old man.
Where I came back to settle down,
It's where they'll put me in the ground:
This is my town.

The above words are the chorus of the blockbuster hit song of 2003, sung by country music entertainers, Eddie Montgomery and Troy Gentry. The entire song captures in graphic detail my memory of Parsons in the 50's as well as the present day. In fact, I keep that CD in the car and every time I go to Parsons to visit my folks, when I hit the City Limit sign, I fire up that bad boy to a fever pitch. When I leave Parsons, I revert to the big hit by The Dixie Chicks, called

"Long Time Gone" which in some ways describes my life even more. As you might assume, if the grandsons are along, they usually beg me to turn it off or at least turn the volume down.

I've often described Parsons as a "poke and plum town"– if you poked your head out the window, you'd be plum out of town. But truth be told, even though the business district was small, it was a thriving little place, especially on Saturdays. Grocery businesses were especially busy: Jack Bell's Grocery, Kenneth Graves Grocery; at one time we had a Jitney Jungle, and are you ready for this– a grocery and feed store called U-Tote-Em.

Jess Readey's Grocery was the most popular spot, inside and out. Inside, folks were buying groceries, mostly on credit. Outside, sitting on the wooden benches, old men in overalls, chewing a plug of tobacco, would spit on you or the sidewalk, whichever got in the line of fire, first. I'll bet John Triplett could've spit tobacco juice ten yards without even trying, especially if he was trying to hit the only un-splattered clean spot on the sidewalk.

The slippery slope of easy money began in 1950 when Frank McNamara created the first credit card–Diners Club. Many more would follow suit but throughout the 50's in Parsons, Tennessee, there were very few credit cards. Now don't get me wrong, folks bought things "on credit." In nearly all of the stores, customers could buy products and then tell the clerk to "put it down" which meant put it in the ledger on their account. When payday came, they made the rounds and either paid off the bill or at least reduced it. A couple of stories regarding such activity need to be included in this segment.

A fellow that I will call Billy Joe Blow worked at the factory, had a house full of kids, and was notorious for not paying his bills, especially at the grocery stores. It was said that only Mr. Readey would let Billy Joe buy groceries on credit. So, every week he would buy a week's supply of groceries and make a minimal payment. Thus, the balance continued to rise until it was clear that BJ would never be able to pay off his account. One payday Mr. Readey asked Billy about his rising unpaid account. The answer was a shock even to Jess Readey who had been in the grocery business for a very long time.

"Mr. Jess, I've been praying about that and the

Lord done told me I didn't have to pay it, that He was gonna take care of it for me."

"Is that right?" retorted Mr. Jess, as he chomped down a little extra hard on his ever present cigar. "Well, you know Billy, the Lord didn't say a word to me about it. But I guess if the Lord told you that, who am I to disagree," whereupon he opened the ledger to Billy Joe Blow's page and wrote, *Paid in full by the Lord.* Then he looked up and said, "Now, let's see if you can stay caught up for a while."

After Billy Joe left the store, someone asked Mr. Jess why he let him get away with such a cock-and-bull story and he replied, "Hell, he wasn't gonna pay it anyway. At least now, his conscience is clear!"

Another story (with all remaining anonymous) involved a man who died while owing another merchant a huge bill. With a long overdue account, he had refused to respond to repeated encouragement to settle his account. After the man's death, it was rumored the merchant opened the ledger to the fellow's page and wrote, "Dead and gone to hell."

➤

At the City Drugs, Dr. Weller, Cozette Hartsfield, Hazel Moore, and Jerry Pratt were standard fixtures. McIllwain's Drug Store was next door where Harold would make a great milk shake for 20 cents or an ice cream soda for 15. You could step over to Harue Gooch's *Do-Drop-Inn* for a plate lunch.

In those days, folks shopped at home. Only a few went to Jackson. Parsons had an abundance of dry goods stores: *R. W. White, Palmer and Adair, Colwick's, Houston's, and Connie Maxwell's,* which begs the question, whatever happened to Dry Goods Stores? The merchandise is still sold but nobody calls them that anymore.

Mr. C.A. Palmer, who along with his wife, co-owned *Palmer and Adair Dry Goods,* was a beloved character who had taught school for many years and was an icon of the absent-minded professor. It was reported that he once walked home from the store forgetting that he had driven to work. But the best story about his mental lapses was the time he intended to spit in the fireplace and throw his socks in the closet... you guessed it, he spit in the closet and threw his socks in the fire!

Which reminds me of the woman who went to the ear doctor because she had lost her hearing aid. During the exam, the doctor pulled something gummy out of her ear.

"What in the world have you been putting in your ear? It looks like a suppository!"

"Oh my God," she exclaimed, "Now I know where I put my hearing aid!"

Meanwhile, back to people and places in downtown Parsons. Just past *Barrett's Jewelry* was *Boaz Tire Store* and across the street was *Melvin King's Shoe Shop. Connie Black's Used Car Lot* was in there, too. (I wonder if Parsons was the only little town around with two men named *Connie*– Connie Maxwell and Connie Black?)

Taxi Drivers and Bootleg Whiskey

There were several cab drivers always around the main intersection, who could be seen in that area, day or night. It was common to hear one of those guys yell at the top of his lungs, "Taxi cab. Anywhere in the world for a half." Little did we know that wasn't half a dollar, it was half a gallon. And he wasn't buying, he was selling. Taxis were big business in those days with all that massive tourism and all!!!

Well, in case you haven't figured it out, some of the taxi drivers were the local bootleggers. They weren't the only ones, by any means, but they did a large share of the business. Decatur County was, is, and likely always will be a "dry county" which meant hard liquor could not be legally sold within the county boundaries. But, beer was permissible; therefore, there were numerous honky tonks and beer joints that had a legitimate license to sell beer. Parsons was "dry" on both accounts. Did that mean hard liquor was not sold in Parsons and Decatur County? No– just wasn't sold legally. What I'm saying is– being a dry municipality and county only meant alcohol wasn't legally available. But make no mistake about it, alcohol in all forms was bought and sold just the same. And man, did they have some ingenuous and creative ways of dispensing their product. One guy had a drive-through window, another had a door bell system where a certain number of rings represented a specific order. And one of them was rumored to have an underground tank filled with white lightning corn whiskey that was tied into his water plumbing system.

When someone placed an order, he put an empty bottle under the water faucet and filled the request– half-pint, pint, fifth, half-gallon, or gallon. Is that clever, or what? If he had put that ingenuity into a legitimate business, he might have made a huge impact on the world. Well, maybe he did anyway– who am I to judge?!

So, I think you get the picture– some of the taxi drivers did a lot of the bootlegging business in Parsons and Decatur County. And it was quite a thriving business, indeed. Those who were into imbibing would drive through town, and with a series of hand signals, place an order. The taxi driver would respond with hand signals, and in short order, the two would meet on a country road with a bottle and money being exchanged between vehicles. As slick as you please and steady as clock work, another "dry county" free-enterprise-supply-and-demand business transaction had been completed.

➤

Decatur County Southern English

As with most rural areas, Decatur County has always had it's own lingo and colloquialisms. Still does, for that matter. Hopefully always will. One of the things I truly love about coming home to my roots is hearing those familiar words and phrases, especially from the older folk. They say things like–

"He's making a doctor"
    Translation: he's a medical student
"They're giving rain"
    Translation: the weather forecast predicts rain
"Taking a headache"
    Translation: a headache is forthcoming
"Slap dab in the middle"
    Translation: at the very center of whatever
"I'm satisfied"
    Translation: I'm confident it's the total truth
"Gotta do some rat killin"
    Translation: to do any job that has to be done
"Flusterated"
    Translation: to be perturbed (flustered) and baffled
    (frustrated) at the same time– thus flusterated
"Wadin"
    Translation: was not
" Ain't no 'count"
    Translation: unable to perform normally
"I'll be there direc-ly"
    Translation: after a slight postponement
"Going to town"
    Translation: doing something in a hurry
"Need to see a man about a dog"
    Translation: having an urge to use the bathroom
"Making water"
    Translation: following that urge
"Anybody cudda told you that"
    Translation: how could you be so stupid
"The North wind will make you sick."
    Translation: the North wind will make you sick
"Looking pretty piert"
    Translation: appears energetic and spry
"Just tolable"
    Translation: just barely getting by
"It's too cold to snow"
    Translation: it's too cold to snow
"Right Smart"
    Translation: in abundance

So, with the aforementioned parlance being clearly fixed in your mind, listening in on a typical conversation between two old timers from Decatur County might go something like this:

"Hear ya been sick?"

"Yeah, it's been flusterating. I was out in that North wind yesterday and it gave me a cold."

"Well, you're lucky you didn't get wet, they were giving rain. But as usual, they missed it."

"Yeah, I heard they were giving rain. But I was satisfied they'd miss it."

"They miss it a right smart, ya know what I mean?"

"Weathermen ain't no count. Dangdest thang I ever seen, they wrong half the time and still keep their job."

"You right 'bout that. Now me and you, if we was to mess up half the time, we'd be sent to the house. You understand what I'm saying?!"

"Ain't it the truth. Them weathermen will say 'partly cloudy with a 50% chance of rain!' Why, anybody coulda told you that!"

"Yeah, and they get paid for it."

"A right smart, I reckon."

"I'm satisfied they do. Not as much as that old Smith boy's gonna make– the one that's making a doctor."

"I thought he was making a preacher?"

"Naw. He's taking doctor training. They tell me he's just going to town."

"Right slap dab in the middle of it, I guess?"

"Well, I'm headed to the house. With that North wind still blowing, I'm taking a headache. Sides, I need to see a man about a dog."

"Yeah, it's kinda chilly, for shore. You better get on in, you ain't looking too piert– I'm just barely tolable, myself."

"That Northwind's made us all sick. If it wadn't too cold to snow, I reckon it would."

"You best get on in the house, I'll finish up my rat killing and be along direc-ly. Think I'll slip out behind the barn and make a little water, my own self."

Service Stations & Churches

In Parsons, during the 50's, there were more service stations (normally called filling stations) than churches. Owners included: Clebe Yates, Rye McIllwain, Jack Maxwell, Herschel Brasher, Herman Townsend, Malcolm Miller, Glenn Wilkins, and Bill Perry. Before the arrival of Interstate 40, Parsons was the Rest Room stop between Memphis and Nashville which was the main reason for all the service stations. With the continuing increase in cars and travelers, traffic got so bad we got our first traffic light. However, until this day, I've never heard a rational explanation as to why it was mounted on a metal pole in the center of the street!

Speaking of service stations, many of us (boys) learned a lot around those service stations, especially in the back of the grease rooms. That's where we got our first dose of grossly distorted sex education by looking at little sexual comic books with x-rated versions of *Blondie and Dagwood, Maggie and Jiggs, Popeye and Olive.* It wasn't *Playboy*, but it was a start. Sometimes we'd buy, sell, and trade these while hiding out between the bales of cotton at the loading dock of the cotton gin on Tennessee Avenue.

Around those service stations, older guys told the younger guys all the stuff we needed to know about sex. Of course, they reveled in exaggeration and falsification. Of one girl who was known to be promiscuous, the older guys said, "She's so wild, she was born with a tattoo!" (The legendary location of which will remain unspoken.)

Speaking of sexual issues– during the 50's sex was quite simply an off-limits subject that was not addressed or discussed, and rarely even mentioned unless it was indirect and the language diffused. Such as: a woman was not said to be *pregnant*, she was *in the family way*, or *PG*, or *in trouble*. To better illustrate this issue, one treasured memory brings a smile to my face.

As was mentioned earlier, my youngest brother, Chris, was born in July of '56 just a few weeks before I turned fifteen. As late as two months before he was born, I still did not know my mother was "in the family way!" By wearing smocks and other loose fitting clothing, she had kept the pregnancy a secret. Why? Because of two things– she was 33 years old, which in those days was considered much too old to be having a baby, and she was afraid that I would be horribly embarrassed and perhaps teased by my schoolmates. So, she waited until school was out to address the issue. Having just finished my paper route, I was sitting at the kitchen table having a quick bite before rushing out to pitch a baseball game.

She began, "Are you really upset with me over what's happening?"

"What's happening?" I questioned.

"My condition," she explained.

"What condition? Are you sick or something?"

"Well, no, I'm not sick. I'm going to have a baby. I thought you probably knew." With that, she sort of sheepishly pointed to her protruding mid-section, which at that point, I could clearly see was "in the family way."

"That's great!" I exclaimed.

"You mean, you aren't embarrassed or ashamed?"

"Lord no! I think it's super. When's the big day?"

"Sometime in July," she said.

"That's terrific. Why haven't you already told me?"

"Well, I just didn't want to upset you."

Now, you must understand that this story in no way is intended to cast a negative light on my mother nor the way she handled this situation. It was just the way it was in that period of time. Sexual oppression was the norm and conversations between parents and children regarding sex, that was such a basic part of life, was taboo. So, we were left to our own devices or vices to get the scoop about the birds and the bees. Which means, using myth, legend, and exaggeration, older kids taught younger kids about sex.

Due to such enormous sexual oppression, when Hugh Hefner published the first issue of *Playboy* magazine in 1954, it was a mind-boggling success. Strangely enough, the people who strongly opposed his magazine were major contributors to its success. But most teenage boys in small towns didn't even know about Playboy for several years. Calendars featuring scantily clad women and pinups were the closest things to nude magazines any of us ever saw.

It is nearly impossible for kids today to understand how the subject of sex was so restricted, controlled, and oppressed in every conceivable manner. Try this on for starters– in the early 50's, there were anti-birth control laws on the books of 30 states, prohibiting everything from the sale of birth control devices to the distribution of birth control literature. If you can believe this, in Connecticut, it was unlawful for a couple to use any sort of contraceptive, meaning birth control was restricted to coitus interruptus or the rhythm method– which for young readers was not about having sex while listening to a boom box!

Then along came one basically unknown and life-changing pioneer in American history who should be revered and immortalized. Seventy-five-year-old Katharine McCormick funded the research that resulted in the creation of the first oral contraceptive. Produced by Searle Pharmaceutical Corp, *Enovid* was approved by the FDA in '57 and the world was introduced to *The Pill*– one more monumental accomplishment of the period known as The 50's.

➤

In addition to Sex Education 101, it was around those service stations that a black kid named "Souse Meat" taught us how to do "the hambone." Or what some people called the Hand Jive– "Hambone, hambone, where ya been, round da world and going agin; whatcha gonna do when you get back? Take a little walk by de railroad track– now hambone." We also learned to Efe or Hootle– "Efe, afe, efe, afe– I'll hootle for a nickel, hootle for a dime, gimme half a dollar and I'll hootle all de time. Efe, afe, efe, afe." Yeah, I can still do all of that stuff and yes again, my grandkids think it's weird. But for a quarter, I'll give you a demo and let you decide for yourself.

Parsons had a typical small Southern town, plain vanilla variety of churches and religious persuasions. As far as we knew, there were no Catholics, Jews, Lutherans, or Episcopalians around. If there were any, they surely kept it quiet. The only Jews we knew were those who owned the local garment factor, Salant & Salant. "Big wheel New York Jews" is what my father and many other factory workers called them. Their chief executives who came to town were Mr. Lipshie and Mr. Gold. I'm not sure anything about the resentment toward the "Big Wheel New York Jews" was anti-semitic. I think the rancor was toward the wealthy bosses and had nothing to do with who they were or where they were from. But as a kid, the message I got was quite clear– being a Jew and being from New York were about as desirable as being what the preachers called a reprobate or a "heathern" whatever the devil that was! God-awful bad is what it was– of that, I was sure.

When the *Sportswear* factory came to Decatur County, it was rumored that a couple of the executives came from "way up North, either from Mitch-agan, Illi-noise, or maybe DE-troit, and they might be Cath-o-licks!" Word got out at one of the beauty shops: "Now you didn't hear it from me, BUT they say two or three of them have I-Talian names so they just might be Cath-o-licks."

Lord have mercy! Cath-o-licks in Decatur County. That's as bad as Yankees in Atlanta. How in the world did they get in?! But if they were Catholic, they kept their faith under a plain brown wrapper and preserved those little mainline protestant churches from outside contamination.

All the churches were actually about the same but thought they were quite different, and, of course, thought their church was the only one that was right, or at least, more right than the others. All the churches were fundamentalists which meant they might not be right but they were never in doubt. The churches included: Methodist, Pentecostal, Church of Christ, Cumberland Presbyterian, and Baptist.

The Baptists practiced baptism by immersion only, pushing their converts completely underwater until every square inch of human flesh was soaking wet. The Baptists seemed to answer the call to missions by having church fights so they could split up and start new churches. They had a pastor one time who had a history of "splitting churches." A dear positive thinking saint said, "It must be his God-given calling. When he pastors a church, it's only one when he comes, but it splits into two before he leaves. Must be the Lord's will." How was that? Hummm.

The Church of Christ dunked their converts, too, but thought that immediate baptism at the time of conversion was essential. When someone responded to a salvation altar call, there was no waiting around for these bad boys to change their minds. Before the convert could finish saying "Save me Jesus," they were about to get their feet wet and every other body part from there on up. The Church of Christ didn't believe in musical instruments in the church, so their singing was all done a capella, which they did very well and extremely impressively. Their theology also included being convinced they were the only ones going to heaven. Seemed like quite a long shot to me.

Now the Methodists were just easy going, don't rock the ecclesiastical boat kind of folks. Their preachers were appointed and usually stayed only two years. Surprisingly, they kept one pastor for several years. When asked about it, one of their leading stewards said, "Actually, we'd prefer not to have a preacher at all. And this fellow is the nearest to nothing we've ever had!" One Methodist minister made quite an impact on me and many others. Because I hung out with some of the Methodist kids, I was invited by their pastor, Rev. Harold McSwain, to go with their youth group to Nashville where I saw my first college football game– Vanderbilt verses Middle Tennessee State University. And to top it off, that evening we went to the old Ryman Auditorium to the Grand Ole Opry where we heard a man who was making his first appearance on that stage. His name? Johnny Cash. His song? "I Walk the Line." We had no idea (neither did anyone else) that we were watching the early stage of a phenomenal career in American musical history. Back to church stuff...

The Presbyterians were of the Cumberland variety. They were just as conservative as the Baptists but seemed to prefer the Presbyterian name. Their Indiana stone church building was quite a nice change from the seemingly sacred all brick buildings of every other denomination.

Parsons also had the Pentecostal Church. We called them Holy Rollers. Their camp meeting assembly sat on a hill overlooking the Tennessee River and was called Holy Roller Hill. They were the charismatics in town whose doctrine included at least two levels of salvation, maybe more. The first level was when you just sorta cleaned up your act. The second level included getting the second blessing, meaning talking in tongues, which they called "getting happy." When you reached the second blessing level, you were sanctified and without sin! Seemed like a stretch to me.

As I said, all the churches were actually about the

same, they just thought they were different. They were basically good folks trying to do a little better with whatever means worked for them. They were in favor of the same things– decency, good will, and common sense. And they were all against the same things– liquor, loose women, and loaded dice for starters. But, more than anything else, every-last-one of them were against one evil that topped all the rest– **modernism**. And by practice, if not definition, modernism was anything that was a change from the way it had always been.

During a Baptist revival meeting, I remember an evangelist getting all riled up about modernism. Said he, "If we don't stop it 'ret nowah,' the way things are going, it won't be long before the Baptists will be a-spranklin' and the Methodists will be using a wet rag!"

All these highly conservative churches used basically the same methodology for motivating their flocks– guilt and fear. After they got through telling you what a rotten, no good, sinner-to-the-bone you were, you felt like the scum of the earth. Then they'd scare the Bejesus out of you by preaching hell so hot you could smell the grease.

After getting the daylights scared out of me from one of those sermons, by a leather-lunged evangelist, I sought out my grandmother Doyle for some counsel. She was a Pentecostal and the "go to" person in the family when you needed to know anything about anything such as: medicine, business, or God. I was about nine at the time.

"Mama Doyle," I said, "Do you have to be baptized to go to heaven?" She was hanging out clothes to dry on an outdoor clothes line, and I was handing them to her. She looked me square in the eyes and said, "Son, I don't rightly know. But no more trouble than it is, I just wouldn't want to take a chance on it."

It would be seven more years before I got around to avoiding taking a chance on it, but I think I knew at that moment that someday I'd take my turn in the baptismal waters, just in case... .

To be honest about it, one of the reasons I waited until I was well past sixteen to officially follow the faith of my heritage was my discomfort and, at times, pure dislike for the preachers I was exposed to. To me, they all seemed so serious about life, living, and the pursuit of happiness that I just couldn't make sense out of what they were saying and how they were living. They all wore dark suits, bland ties with white heavily starched shirts, and were dressed that way day and night. I assumed they slept that way.

I'm sure they were wonderful men (of course, they were all men, since there were no women clergy in those days, except in the charismatic churches where a token number of women were allowed to preach.) No doubt, it was my distorted and immature view, but those men just didn't appeal to me. They preached about love, faith, grace, and hope, but most of them went around looking like they had a sour stomach or a bad case of the eppizutees. They seemed to be terribly upset with the possibility that someone somewhere was having a good time.

Then George Capps came to town. He was pastor of the First Baptist Church during my high school years and he had a profound impact on my life. To me, he was the first preacher I had ever known who had *kuhunas!* (I assume you get my drift.)   It was under his ministry that I decided to take my turn in the baptismal waters, just in case.

Reflecting back on it, I don't know if I really believed the message or just strongly believed in the messenger, but I do know he was a very positive influence in my young life. He died much too early. But if a full life is correctly measured much more by the influence you leave than the years you last, then George Capps lived a very full life, indeed.

There were many people in the First Baptist Church of Parsons that impacted me in a very positive way. Even at the risk of offending some because of being left out, I'd like to name a few. Hobart and

Raymond Townsend and their dear wives, "Miss" Ruth and "Miss" Sophia, who faithfully played the organ and piano respectfully for longer than any of us could count. And there was Ruth Carrington, who I suspect attended more Baptist church meetings over a life-time than any two people combined. She was basically a quiet soul but a straight shooter who could be, er could be, well... a little abrasive at times. No, quite abrasive, actually. But if you *really* knew her, you definitely loved her. I did.

With great fondness, I remember the Bowmans— brother and sister, Barbara and Albert. Who could ever forget Uncle John Tinker, an icon of dignity, integrity, and faith, who prayed the longest prayers you've ever heard. If the pastor called on Uncle John for the invocation, we (kids) were relieved because that meant he wouldn't be asked to give the benediction which meant we might miss lunch.

Annie and Jessie Dodd were regular fixtures and walked to church from their "little rock house on the hill." He was my Sunday School teacher for a time and died much too early. Ralph Smith was a consistent source of support at church and from his place of business— Smithy's Body Shop— and for that, I will be forever grateful. Allie Mae and Billy Stevens were choir members forever; so was Noble Lindsay.

Speaking of music, before the church split, I remember Elbert Barnett leading the singing along with his music teacher wife, "Miss" Bill, at the organ. Elbert had a well-trained slightly operatic voice that was a little too sophisticated for us kids, who thought he sounded a bit strange. I can still hear him singing "Ready," #300 from the Broadman Hymnal. The chorus goes, "Ready to go, ready to stay, ready my place to fill; Ready for service, lowly or great, ready to do His will." Elbert enunciated that word *ready* with great gusto and it came out, "Rrrready to go, rrrready to stay, rrrready my place to fill; Rrrready for service, lowly or great, rrrready to do His will."

When he got to that third "rrrready," we kids would be about to pop. I'd have to bite my lip to keep from giggling. But I'm pretty sure Jay Wallace and Gary Carrington laughed out loud!

Some of the kids played a naughty little game with the hymn book. Not me of course! Okay, maybe I did a time or two! Okay, okay, so I was a regular player– maybe even the instigator more than half the time– are you satisfied now blabbermouth??!!!

Here's how it worked– you flipped through the pages and stopped at random on any given song, then read the title of the song, and immediately uttered the phrase "...between the sheets!" Well, I wanna tell you, to hormone enraged teenagers, it was hilarious!

> "When We All Get to Heaven"
> (...between the sheets!)
> "Must I Go, And Empty Handed?"
> (...between the sheets?)
> "Leaning on the Everlasting Arms"
> (...between the sheets!)

I'm sure you get the picture. It's amazing what teenagers will do to have a little fun in church!

Speaking of the church folk who influenced my life, near the top of the list is sweet and lovable, Sue Carrington. She directed the youth department in Sunday School for more years than she could count and impacted more young people's lives than she'll ever know, including mine. "Miss" Sue didn't just survive the horrible war-time loss of her husband, she lived a beautiful, influential life, in the face of it. With remarkable creativity, patience, and grace, coupled with a winsome personality and infectious smile, young people were attracted to her like bees are drawn to honey. Why? Because she made people feel good about themselves. She definitely gets my vote as one of those who influenced my life the most.

Churches were then and are now a fundamental and rudimentary part of small town life. I'm satisfied that's the way it should be.

Tragedies and More Tragedies

As with all communities during any era, Parsons had its share of tragedies. I remember all too well fierce, residential and commercial fires, deadly tornadoes, like the one that hit Bible Hill, tragic car wrecks involving teenagers and adults, shocking suicides, and catastrophic illnesses. As a kid, some of these affected me more than others, so I decided to include a few of these stories in this volume.

A Mother Does Her Job

For a while, before I started to school, we lived in a duplex apartment on Tennessee Avenue, right across the street from the Herndons– Charlie, Gladys, Doris, Joyce, Bobby, Charles, and Grandma Dodd. Later we moved five houses up the street which means I was around the Herndons throughout my entire childhood.

Charlie operated a local Gulf service station right in the center of town. One Saturday night after he had locked up, he went into the backroom at the service station and shot himself.

With responsibilities for kids ranging in age from pre-school to junior high and a mother to boot, Gladys Herndon had a plate full. And, without question, Gladys Herndon was one of the heroes of my youth. Working two jobs– head cook in the high school cafeteria and short order cook at the Snack Bar at night– she raised those four children virtually by herself. Without a car, she walked everywhere she went and to top it off, she always had a smile, laughed a lot, and to me, seemed totally at peace. Wow– what an example of taking whatever hand life deals you and "getting it done." During a large portion of my youth, I spent a lot of hours in the swing on their front porch talking sports with Bobby and laughing with Gladys. Yep, she was definitely one of my childhood heroes.

The Death of Harvey Smith

"Wake up Don, Harvey died last night. Gid's coming up to play with you." Those are the words I remember my mother whispering with a quivering voice sometime in the year 1952. Along with Gid, Harvey's brother, I was in sixth grade.

Harvey Smith was an All American kid– athletic, good student, clean living, dedicated Christian, great personality.   He was the second oldest of four brothers and a sister of the Hazel and Hardin Smith family–   one of Decatur County's most respected families. They were all great kids– David, Harvey, Larry, Gail, and Gid– and Harvey held his own with a charismatic spark that was noticeable to all. He was a good athlete and played on the high school football team where he sustained a leg injury that wouldn't heal. After a long time, it was finally diagnosed as cancer. His leg was amputated but he still died six months later at age eighteen.

When I awakened to my mother's words, I felt a sense of intense anxiety. What would I say? What would we do? How could I relate to a school mate whose brother had just died? The Smiths lived directly behind us on the next street over. As I saw Gid walking up the road, I remember feeling a tightness in my stomach and throat as I walked out in the back yard to meet him. What would I say? What would we do? These are tough questions for adults, much more for an eleven-year-old! Turning to my mother in desperation while holding back the tears, I said, "What do I say to him?"

She replied, "Just tell him you're sorry and then play ball with him."

Walking out through the carport, I followed her suggestion and picked up the basketball and headed straight toward the backboard and hoop on the cedar tree. "Hi Gid, sorry 'bout Harvey."

Gid nodded without speaking. After a brief pause, I bounced the ball to him and said, "Wanna play a game of horse?" He nodded again and I said, "It's your shot." He smiled and made the basket.

More than fifty years later, with several degrees, and thousands of hours of counseling experiences under my belt, I doubt that I could improve on that exchange. When family and friends are in a crisis, most of the time, the best thing we can do for them is to be *present*. Trying to come up with something inspirational, clever, or soothing in the face of tragedy will more often than not, fall on deaf ears at best, and be insulting at the worst. Just being present is about as good as it gets. As a kid, I didn't know that and for me, just "showing up" was as much as I could do. Many years later, I concluded that was as much as I needed to do.

Fire In The Lodge

Several tragedies involved fire. By far, the most memorable for me began shortly before 6:00 p.m. on December 29, 1956. That's when the Masonic Lodge, which was located on the second floor of a building in the very heart of downtown Parsons, caught fire. The siren blew, and as usual, the whole town knew it and many went out "to watch the fire." The all volunteer fire department was, to say the least, not very efficient or professional. But they tried hard– gave their time and sometimes risked their lives to saved others. But most of the time the fires were rather insignificant with very little danger to anyone. At any rate, on this particular fire call, that was not the case.

Riding my SIMPLEX motorcycle to find the fire, I was surprised to discover it was right in the center of

town, in the Masonic Lodge hall, which was on the
second floor of an old building in the little business
intersection. Underneath the lodge was a restaurant
called "The Do Drop Inn" and next door was a
women's clothing store called "Annie's Dress Shop."

At first there wasn't much fire to it, just smoke
seeping around the windows and out the opened door
to the stairwell leading up to the second floor.
Firemen were spraying water up the stairwell but no
one had actually gone into the hall itself. A fellow by
the name of James Goff placed a ladder on the side of
the building, climbed it, broke a window and began
spraying water inside the lodge. I can still see him
now with his leg hooked over one of the ladder rungs
about fifteen feet above the ground.

Everything seemed to be getting under control.
People were wandering around the buildings. Some
were busy removing merchandise from "Annie's
Dress Shop" which was taking on some water from
overhead. Others were helping HaRue Gooch move
equipment from "The Do Drop Inn" which was also
taking on water. And then it happened.

Standing perhaps twenty feet from the building, in
front of Uncle Clebe Yates' Esso service station, I was
looking directly at James Goff when the top of the
building made a double belching sound. Separated by
only an instant, the second explosion brought the
building down. I mean the entire front wall and side
wall came apart. Tons of brick rained down, along
with James Goff. He literally jumped out of the ladder

and away from the exploding brick. God only knows
how he came out of that with only a broken leg.

On the ground below, people ran for their lives,
myself included, as bricks were falling everywhere and
bouncing and rolling once they hit the ground.

A fellow– the Otis of Mayberry local drunk who
will go unnamed– was hit on the head with a brick.
I can still see him crawling on his hands and knees
with blood trickling down his face, crying, "Oh my
God, it's the end of the world!"

Clebe Yates had tried for years to help him take
control of his life and stop drowning himself in booze.
So, he used the opportunity to try once again.

"No, it's not the end of the world. But the devil
just nearly got your butt. Don't you think this would
be a good time to give your heart to the Lord?" I

don't remember it making any difference with "Otis" but at least it was a good try.

Obviously it wasn't the end of the world for all, but it was for two who were literally "hit with a ton of bricks." Judge, Madison (Pig) Smith was killed. Owner of Bell's Grocery, Jack Bell, which was just across the street, was covered with bricks but refused to go to the hospital in the first ambulance because he didn't think his injuries were serious enough to take someone else's place. He died a few days later from internal injuries.

Our classmate, Marijon Young, was literally buried with bricks and mortar and was dug out by a fellow named Dorsey Battles. She was seriously injured with a broken pelvis and broken hand along with major head injuries that required more stitches than anyone could count. She was unable to walk for eight weeks. According to some people, "She was one of the lucky ones." I guess so. Thank God, she recovered and never looked the worst for wear and was just as pretty as ever. Still is.

Back to the fire. When the building exploded, as you might have guessed, that's when the real fire started. Once the fire got air, that old building began to cook. The fire apparently started from a faulty gas heater and was burning lightly until the water through the window stopped the fire but not the gas leak. Once the building filled with gas, it didn't take long for a spark to find it and then the explosion. And the real fire was underway. Now that whole section of town was in danger. Flames were shooting skyward at what looked like twenty-five feet high and people were panicking.

By now, without any central leadership to give direction, what seemed like hundreds of people were scurrying around in all directions helping the injured, moving furnishings and merchandise from stores, fighting the fire. And it was cold– very cold.

Almost immediately, I grabbed a fire hose to help one of the volunteer firemen. We hooked it up to a fire hydrant about 30 yards away between the homes of Mr. and Mrs. Wes White and Mr. and Mrs. Ralph Jennings and began shooting water into the blaze. After quite some time, without gloves, or sufficient clothing, I was feeling numb from the freezing temperatures. Finding someone to take my place, I jumped on my SIMPLEX and went home to put on the clothing I used to carry papers during wet winter weather– insulated boots, rain suit, rubber gloves. Much to my mother's chagrin, I went back to "fight the fire." It was like I had to do it. Feeling awful about what had happened, it seemed the only thing that gave it some balance for me was to be involved in the rescue effort.

As a member of the high school basketball team that had a home game that night, for the only time in my athletic career, I missed a ball game. Even though I was not a first teamer, I did play some and I remember thinking that Coach Southerland would be really mad. But at some level, I knew it didn't matter.

And of course, he wasn't mad and it didn't matter.

The fire lasted well into the night but the other buildings were saved and there was no more loss of life. Holding a fire hose till I was exhausted, I can still remember standing for a part of the time by myself, nearly in the dark, feeling very emotional– lonely, sad, and at times on the verge of tears– but refusing to turn loose of that fire hose. Not unlike some other tragedies of my childhood, this one may have sealed the deal of conscious awareness that during a crisis I could do something to make a difference. I wasn't about to give up that feeling.

Speaking of fires. The volunteer fire department had its problems. One night the fire truck got out of control and drove through the front of The Farmers Bank. *The News Leader* ran a picture with the fire truck sitting in the lobby of the bank. The words, "Solid as a Rock" were still visible on the front wall.

The Passing of Opal Maxwell

One of the tragedies that impacted me the most was the death of Mrs. Opal Maxwell–" Miss" Opal to us kids. The Maxwells lived two houses down from us on Tennessee Avenue. They were a family of six– Elven, Opal, Yancy, Joevelyn, Ralph and Ronnie– and every one of them were just the nicest people you'd ever want to meet. The two girls were a few years older than me; Ralph and I were only a few months apart; Ronnie was a year younger than my sister, Sheila. I loved all of them dearly– still do.

When I was six or seven years old, Yancy and Jo taught me to ride a bicycle and before I got the hang of it, after a rather dramatic wreck, helped with some first aid. I knocked the top off a bare-footed big toe while trying to stop the bike before hitting the fence in their back yard. They took me and my bleeding toe to their mother where Miss Opal poured some coal oil (kerosene) in a tin cup and made me put my foot in it! Then Yancy and Jo wrapped it in a small strip of cloth torn from an old bed sheet, and tied a string around it. That's when I knew I had a crush on those girls! Later, I would get a crush on Ruth Dodson, Elsie Jordan, Doris and Joyce Herndon and all the other "older girls" in the neighborhood. All of us played on the cotton bales at the loading platform of Freeman Wilson's cotton gin on the corner and in the Cedar Grove woods, and we climbed the cedar trees in our backyard playing Tarzan and Jane.

Even though Ronnie was nine years younger than me, I remember him as a really neat kid who was enjoyable to be around and as the baby of the family, a treat for his brother and sisters.

Ralph and I had been friends from about age five when we moved into our house that his master carpenter father had built. There are a hundred "Ralph stories" that could be told. A few will do.

When we were about seven or eight years old, Ralph and I decided to build a dog house. Not just an ordinary dog house, mind you, but a super duper dog house, with pitched roof, shingles and the whole nine yards. Well, somehow, someway, before that project was completed, Ralph got nailed up between the rafters. Actually, he just turned his head the wrong way, thought he was stuck, and began screaming bloody murder! No matter what I did or said, he wouldn't turn his head in the direction required to get free. Finally, determined to cut him loose, I picked up a handsaw, put it down beside his head. That's when his screams picked up about two decibels. Persisting, I finally cut through the rafter and he vacated the doghouse for ever. For some reason he always blamed me for getting stuck in the doghouse, saying I nailed it up around him— not sure why?!

Another story needs to be added. Ralph and I once built a boat to use in Dr. Hufstedler's stock pond in the Cedar Grove Woods. Spent two or three days planning, measuring, sawing, nailing, calking. Finally

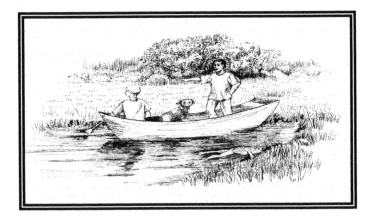

got it finished and carried it to the pond for its maiden voyage. Put it in the water, got in it, and shoved off.

Faster than we could yell, "We've got a leak!" it sank. So much for boat building.

During the same period of time, Ralph and I were in the Cedar Grove Woods with our BB guns shooting at rabbits, squirrels, and birds, but killing more time than game. All at once we saw this incredible contraption in the sky, moving slowly and deliberately over Cedar Grove. Frantically, Ralph yelled, "It's an atomic bomb! I know it is. It's the end of the world." Ralph swears I'm the one who made those statements. But I'm sure it was him. Well, almost sure. After all, who's writing this story, anyway?! In case you haven't already guessed, it was, of course, the Goodyear blimp.

Back to the main reason for writing this piece. Miss Opal was a wonderfully kind and loving woman who would do anything in the world to help her family and everyone else. But sadly, she suffered from an illness that left her tense and anxious and she would go into deep depressions. She was said to "have bad nerves." Regrettably, in those days treatment for such problems was very limited. On more than one occasion, she tried to self- destruct. In November of '56, she succeeded and died a couple of days later.

Yancy had already graduated from high school, Joevelyn was a senior, Ralph was a freshman, and Ronnie was in first grade. It was a horrible tragedy for our little community on Tennessee Avenue and even the whole town of Parsons. But it was a devastating experience for those children and for that husband and father– Mr. Elven. But he made his adjustments and went on with his life of being a fine father and carpenter. The way he handled the loss is one part of this tragedy that made a huge impression on me.

A few months after Miss Opal's death, I was helping my mother hang out clothes to dry on an outdoor clothesline. That's when she said something I will never forget.

"Well, I believe Elven is gonna be alright."

"How do you know that?"

"Listen."

What I heard was someone whistling. Looking around, I spotted the whistler, Mr. Elven, doing some roof repair on Henry Greenway's house just behind us. We looked at each other and smiled. As clear as a bell, he was whistling *Amazing Grace*.

At that moment, I knew two things: Mr. Maxwell was a man of integrity, character, and strength and my mother was a very wise and observant woman.

Small Town Fun, Tall Tales
&
Other Stories

Parsons didn't have a lot of activity for young people growing up in the 50's– probably not a lot different in the present. Sometimes we went to see the legendary haunted houses, visited an occasional graveyard, went to Busseltown to look at Lady's Bluff where folklore recounted that a scorned woman had jumped to her death into the deep waters of the Tennessee River.

In a similar vein, on a pretty regular basis, we drove by the house where the old lady lived who had been left at the altar when she was young and every night since then she had stood at the window looking out to see if her lover would return. If you looked closely, you could see her shadow on the window shade– at least that's the way the story went.

Stealing Watermelons

One of our more daring summertime amusements was stealing watermelons. I'd like to minimize it by calling it something else, but no matter how you slice it (no pun intended), it was stealing watermelons, plain and simple. On a hot summer night with a carefully laid plan, we would go out to some farmer's watermelon patch. The driver would stop the car, let the pickers out, and come back later to pick up the guys and the melons. We'd laugh and head straight to the city park where we'd burst the watermelons and eat nothing but the heart– dug out with our bare hands. It was heaven. Like I said, it didn't take a lot to entertain us.

On one occasion, a clever farmer put a sign up in his patch which was designed to eliminate the thievery. It read: "ONE melon in this patch has been poisoned." Since only the farmer knew which one, he thought this would eliminate the would-be watermelon thieves. However, much to his dismay, one morning when he checked out his watermelon patch, he was greeted with a sickening sight. The sign had been slightly altered. The word ONE had been crossed out and replaced with the word TWO and thus now read: "TWO melons in this patch have been poisoned."

On another watermelon caper, the stealers got their due. We had been dropped off at a particular spot where "the melons are huge and sweet but Old Elwood really watches, so we have to be extra quiet."

Crossing a creek and climbing a fence, we were making our way through a corn field, headed for the patch that was just over the hill, when to our total shock, we were greeted with the sound of a 12 gauge shotgun that rained pellets down all over the corn field, including us. We all hit the dirt. The moon was full and bright. Wearing a white shirt, I took it off to avoid being spotted so easily.

Another gun shot rang out and then a booming voice, "Damn you smart ass kids. You're not gonna steal my watermelons and get away with it. You little bastards, I'll blow your asses off! " He fired again.

A couple of guys started running, jumping corn rows and fences back through the woods. Houston Barrett and I stayed on our bellies crawling through the corn rows and whispering about our plans to get away. After a few minutes, (which seemed like hours) we heard laughter, then more laughter. Finally, we heard the sweetest words of the night, "We scared the crap out of you guys, didn't we?"

The whole thing had been a setup. Some of our group had planned it and had carried it off to perfection. Even some of those in the field had been in on the plot. We all had a good laugh and went back to town together, all except one kid who ran through the woods all the way back to Parsons. He was skinned and scratched from sawbriars and didn't know until the next day that the whole experience had been a hoax. Rather than give his grandkids some teasing ammo, his identity will remain a secret.

We took a lot of tormenting over the next several days and it made quite a story for our summertime boredom. Strangely enough, even though it was all a prank, I never stole another watermelon.

Bisbees and the County Fair

During the 50's, (as already pointed out in graphic detail) we didn't have a wide variety of extraordinary entertainment in Parsons and Decatur County. Well, maybe some of it was unusual but not, shall we say, "culturally challenging." However, two things stand out in my memory that were exceptions extra ordinaire– the *Bisbees* in the spring, and the *Decatur County Fair* in the fall.

Bisbees was a traveling vaudeville show that played small towns all across the region. Staying for a three-day run, they had a giant tent that seated probably 200 people but to us kids, it seemed like it would hold thousands. They had musicians, jugglers, magicians, slap stick comedians, dancing girls, and every show was topped off by a short three-act stage play. They sold cotton candy, snow cones, popcorn, and boxes of chewy taffy-like candy that contained prizes and at least one of those boxes had a "grand prize" that wasn't much but seemed like a lot.

When the Bisbees came to town they would recruit a few teenage boys to help with setting up the tent and elementary boys to distribute posters that were nailed to utility poles and placed in store windows. Payment came in the form of a couple of free tickets. Some of the guys skipped school to work for Bisbees, but I don't remember them ever getting in trouble with the truant officer– Mr. Obie Hendrix.

Now it's important for you to get this picture because as strange as it may seem, Bisbees coming to Parsons electrified the community. I mean folks got excited and with bated breath talked about the traveling vaudeville show. "You goin' to Bisbees tonight?" "Yeah, I been saving up for it." "You going?" "If mama will pay me what she owes me, I am." "How bout you, Bubba, you going?" "Naw, don't have enough money." "Ah, man!"

Then there was the annual county fair in the fall which brought a week of fun and festivities. For many of us, the agricultural side of the fair was okay but the real "show" was the carnival! I'm talking the rides– carousel, ferris wheel, tilt-a-whirl, flying tubs, giant swings, and the bullet. Then there were the game booths to try to win a teddy bear, and the side shows that had such things as– Two-headed Snake, Half-man/Half ape, Sword Swallower, Smallest Woman in the World, 2,000 Year Old Mummy, Woman with a Full Beard, and many many more.

Then way over on the outskirts of the main carnival midway– The Girlie Show. "Come one, come all, see Little Egypt. She walks, she talks, she crawls on her belly like a reptile. If you're going, let's go now. One hard half-a-dollar pays the way."

Some of us boys would walk around at a safe distance   pretending not to be looking or even noticing what was going on. But out of the corner of our eyes we were soaking it all in. Looking to see which older boys and men were going inside to take a closeup look at Little Egypt.

"Get on away from here boys– this is a show for MEN only," shamed the hawker. "So, come on all you *real men* and let Little Egypt ring your bell, pull your chain, and wind you up tighter than a banjo string. If you're going, let's go now. One hard half-a-dollar pays the way."

Beyond all of the above, one of things about the fair that was a huge benefit to high school juniors and seniors was having concessions booths. It was through those efforts that a large portion of the money for the senior trip was raised. It taught us the value of teamwork and cooperation for a common cause. In my opinion, the value of those money making experiences was immeasurable.

Betcha Can't Top That!

Typical of small towns and rural America is the long standing traditional tall tale. Men in court squares and country stores, trade knives and swap lies. Always told as the truth (in fact, most of them start with some semblance of actuality) but then a little embellishment sets in to produce a little better story and before you know it a tall tale is born.

One such story involved my brother, Mickey.

Right out of high school, he had a truck route for TOM's PEANUTS. In fact, that's a story in itself that's worth repeating so I'll digress for a moment.

On one occasion, Mickey told me that he liked his work but was bothered to tell people he was "a peanut peddler." So, I suggested that when people asked about his work, he could respond, "I'm a distribution manager for Tom's Brazilian Herbs." Mickey said he liked that a lot and would try it. Sometime later, I asked him how his new title was faring.

"Well, I did like you said and told this guy that I was a distribution manager for Tom's Brazilian Herbs, and he said, "What the hell is that?" And I said, "Peanut Peddler." (So much for big brother's advice!)

Anyway, back to the original story. Mickey was in a country store in Perry County distributing his herbs when he over-heard a conversation involving several old men who were sitting around a pot-bellied stove, telling stories regarding *terrible things tornadoes can do.*

Stories such as these usually started with some element of truth, but time and hyperbole had taken a huge toll and each story got a little more outrageous than the one before. Here's the way it went.

One man leaned back, shoved his hands down in his Duckhead overalls, and laid it on. By the way, for those who aren't really familiar with overalls, they were the uniform of choice for the majority of country farmers and they lived up to their name because they could be worn "over all or over nothing at all." In the winter they were worn over longjohns, in the summer those Duckheads might be all that man was wearing between himself and the Lord. Meanwhile, back to the tall tale tornado stories.

"Back in '39 down in Alabamer, when I was just a kid of a boy, a house got blowed away, clean off the foundation, took it two mile down the road, set er

down and never broke a dish." The contest was on.

Spitting his tobacco juice in the direction of the spit bucket, the next fable donor embarked, "You think that's something? Well, let me tell you one. After a bad twister came through Marked Tree, Arkansas, we found a corn stalk six inches deep in a white oak tree. Yes sir, shore was– seen it with my own eyes. That's how Marked Tree got its name. Yes sir, it shore is…" It got deeper.

"After thatun hit Bible Hill in '52, my wife's half-wit cousin, Eugene, found a broom straw sticking through a 2 by 4."

"Well, that's all hard to believe and all," said an old man sitting next to the stove. He had just finished rolling a cigarette, licked the paper to make it stick, and was putting the Prince Albert back in his jumper pocket. He struck a wooden match with his thumb nail, fired up his roll-your-own cigarette, took a deep drag and continued, "but nothing like that nasty tornader that came through the south end of the county when I was still a youngun. Yes sirree, that was a doozie."

He paused a bit to increase the drama and then continued to drawl out every word and syllable. "Did a turble lot of damage, you understand. Blowed away houses, tore up crops, killed folks. But I think the worst part about it was what it did to Uncle Frank's white mule." His timing was perfect. He sighed and then took another long drag on the Prince Albert.

With bated breath, someone finally said, "What'd

it do to the mule, Earl?"

"Well sir, that mule was missing for several days before Uncle Frank finally found it down in the holler in a gallon jug!"

According to Mickey, that about wound things up for the tornado tall tales– at least for that day.

➤

Granddaddy Tells a Story

There's no way I could finish the story telling part of this volume without including a couple from my father, Maxie Doyle. Periodically, the grandchildren will talk him into telling one of his standards. Even though they've heard them many times, it's still a treat to "get Granddaddy to tell a story." They're the same ones I heard as a kid and yet they're just as funny to me now as they were then. Here goes... just as Maxie would tell them.

Story #1–

Two fellows were going out to do some rabbit hunting– one was a local guy, the other was his friend from the city. They stopped the pickup in front of the farmhouse and the local fellow went in to get clearance from the old farmer to hunt his fields. The farmer gladly gave permission but then made a request. "I've got an old no-count mule out there that's feeble and sick and in bad shape. He needs to be put out of his misery. You'll see him in that first pasture on your way to where you're gonna hunt. If you'll just stop and shoot that old mule for me, I'd appreciate it. I just would feel kinda bad doing it myself– the old nag has been good to me and I just don't have the heart to shoot him myself. But if you'll do it for me, later on today I'll get the tractor and drag him off in the woods."

"Be glad to," said the would-be hunter. Walking back to his truck, he decided to pull a fast one on his city slicker friend. He got in the truck and started raving that the old man had **refused** to let them hunt. Laying it on thick, he said, "That makes me so mad, I think I'm just gonna shoot his danged old mule." With that, he slammed on the brakes, jumped out of the truck, pulled the shotgun from the rack, stepped out into the field, and shot the mule. But before he could turn to see the look on his friend's face, two more shots rang out. When he turned around, much to his shock, his city slicker friend exclaimed, "Well, it made me mad, too, so I shot two of his cows!"

Story #2– again, in Maxie's own words.

A couple of old farm hands (Woodrow and Claude) had a daily ritual. Every morning, Woodrow picked up Claude on the way to the field and every day without fail, Claude bummed chewing tobacco off Woodrow. The tobacco was old homegrown leaf tobacco that Woodrow kept in the pocket of his jumper coat.

One morning Woodrow picked up some discarded tobacco that was in a basket under the chicken roost. (If you get the picture, that meant the chicken droppings had frequently hit the tobacco leaves. But it had dried and wasn't very visible.) Woodrow rolled up some of the chicken dropping contaminated leaves nice and tight and put them in his coat pocket.

He picked up Claude and they headed to the field and just like clockwork, Claude was right on cue.

"Woodrow, could I get a chaw of tobaker?"

"Help yourself," Woodrow nodded, whereupon Claude reached over in Woodrow's jumper pocket, pulled out a leaf, rubbed it up, made a wad out of it, and poked it in his jaw.

After a couple of minutes, Claude said, "Woodrow, do you smell chicken shit?"

"Nah, I don't smell nothing."

Another minute passed. "Are you sure you don't smell chicken shit? Man, I smell it strong!"

"Nah, I don't smell nothing," Woodrow said, still keeping a straight face.

Then another minute went by and Claude blurted

out, "Woodrow, I'm tellin' you there's some chicken shit somewhere in this truck. I can smell it so strong, I can taste it!!!!"

There's no way to count the number of times I've heard my father tell that story but I laugh just as hard every time. So do the grandchildren and now even the great grandchildren. As of this writing, at age 86, he's still going strong and still telling those stories.

➤

People in Parsons

In the 50's, in between whittling and swapping knives and lies, old men played a lot of checkers and dominoes in Colwick Square. All the pieces were

wooden. If there was a shortage of checkers, coke tops filled in very nicely. Old women talked about those old men playing checkers, whittling, and swapping knives and lies– usually not in endearing terms!

During the 50's, at his daddy's service station, Gaylon Yates serviced cars on roller skates. It was a novelty, to the say the least, and always brought a lot of attention. On day Gaylon was pumping gas for someone who was passing through town and the man said, "Is Parsons a progressive little town?"

Gaylon replied, "Not really."

"Do you have a Chamber of Commerce?"

"Yeah," said Gaylon, "we've got a Chamber of Commerce alright, but they seem to have a lot more chamber than they do commerce."

Speaking of commerce and progress– Tom Jennings, our local photographer, made more pictures than anyone could possibly count. Shorty Conger would make frequent arrests on out of town folks until one of the real policemen would stop him. Big Boy Moore was always around– either working or watching. Dumb Dolly Sparks was a standard at Malcolm Miller's Gulf station, and you could always find Sleepy Miller working, at least part of the time, for Ralph Smith at *Smitty's Body Shop and Garage* (a standard in Parsons for as long as anybody can remember.) If you were down on that end of town, you could also take a look at Mr. Bob Smith's 1913 Ford which was his pride and joy.

Doug Hays was a big supporter of high school athletics, so was Mr. Pevahouse and Red Gilbreath. Mr. Carl Partin would find whatever you needed at Boaz Hardware. If you were over on the Bible Hill Road, you could stop by Marchbanks little grocery for an RC Cola and a Moon Pie. I can still hear Mr. Lester Marchbanks say, "Howdy GentleBoys. Let's have nothing but silence and very little of that!"

Joe Marshall was the Scout Master for Troop 29 and did more for Scouting and more to shape the lives of numerous young boys than anybody could measure. Shortly before he died in a nursing home in Orlando, Florida, I wrote to him telling him of my appreciation for all he had meant to me in my youth and reminded him of all the trips we took in his old blue '51 Plymouth. In scrawled handwriting, he answered, "That old Plymouth was a good old girl!"

In my letter to him, I mentioned I could still see him in the Scout House on Water Tank Hill, hanging by his heels from the overhead rafters, just to show us he could. Each time Troop 29 got a new member, he had to do the "hanging by the heels trick" cause the new kids wouldn't believe it until they could see it.

Late in life, due to severe diabetes, both Mr. Marshall's legs were amputated below the knees. In his letter to me, he wrote about hanging by his heels by saying, "I'd have a hard time doing that now! Ha Ha!" (I still have that treasured letter.)

The Barbers

The City Barber Shop had three barbers– Osco Taylor, Rudolph Raines, and Coy Sullivan. They cut standard haircuts for the older men, and flattops for the boys and sold Butch wax, Vaseline hair tonic, Jeris hair brushes, and treated everybody with dignity, respect and good humor. They were just three of the nicest men you'd ever want to meet. If I concentrate, I can still remember the distinctly pleasant smell of that shop and I can hear each one of them in their own patented voice saying, "Next!"

Speaking of the flattop– that was the style of choice for the majority of teenagers and young men. And we were quite particular about having our flattops cut just right. One day a boy came back to the shop and gently complained to Uncle Osco that his flattop was crooked. As Osco inspected the crooked haircut, he put his hands on each side of the boy's face and tilted his head slightly to one side. Then in a very serious voice he said, "Why son, all you gotta do is just hold your head a little to the right, and it'll look perfect!" As the kid's eyes widened to the size of silver dollars, Osco let out a big laugh, and promptly moved the kid into his chair where he fixed the tilted flattop haircut.

Everybody loved the City Barber Shop but more than a few were a little dismayed when they raised the haircut price to sixty-five cents.

Osco Taylor died in 2003 at age 96. A few months before he died, I went to see him in the Parsons nursing home. It was a Sunday afternoon and he was lying on his bed, fully dressed, but taking a nap. Gently, I put my hand on his leg and shook it enough to awaken him. When he opened his eyes, I said, "How 'bout a haircut." He replied, "You're next!"

My mother was with me and had visited Osco on a regular basis so he knew her but couldn't figure out who I was. Having only seen him a few times in more than 40 years, it took a lot of coaxing before he finally recognized me. Then he said, "Well son, you shore have gotten a lot wider!" What a terrific response. In more than four decades since I had seen him on a regular basis, I had, indeed, gotten a lot wider!

The Doctors

As with many a small town, Parsons was blessed with some good country doctors. Dr. Hubert Conger, Dr. L.E. Luna, and Dr. Ingram were the three standards for all of my youth. They did it all– sewed up wounds, delivered babies, administered drugs, did minor surgeries, and still made some house calls. You name it and they did it.

Now and then another physician would come to town but usually for a short time only. I figure it was due to the phenomenal work load. No matter where they went, night or day, they were on call. At the football game, "Doc, this ear's 'bout to drive me crazy." At church, "Doc, would you come out and take a look at my Susie, she's throwing up something that looks like cat hair." On the street, "Doc, I know you ain't no dog doctor, but Old Blue's sick to death. Can you give him something?" Never any relief. And it's amazing how they handled it.

One new doctor came to town, a fellow by the name of McInerney. Due to the overload of the other three, his practice took off. But in a matter of months, one day with a waiting room full of patients, Dr. McInerney went into his personal office, closed

the door, put a pistol in his mouth and killed himself.
I was quite young and never heard any of the details.
Everything was sorta hush hush. The older folks just
said it was a terrible thing. I understood that.

Dr. Hufstedler was the local dentist and Dr. Davis
did optometry. Both had more work than they could
do and did it forever, it seemed to me.

Dr. Conger was our main family doctor and was a
fine man whom I admired greatly. He thought I was
going to go off to school and "make a doctor" and
he'd often say to me, "Donnie, you take a long look at
doing General Practice rather than a highfalutin'
specialty– the GP's are coming back." And they did,
too, in the form of what we know today as Family
Practice. But I didn't go very far in pursuing a career
in medicine– college chemistry and higher math put
an end to that in a hurry! Even though I didn't
officially give up the idea of medicine until my senior
year in college, it was during the first semester of my
freshman year that I figured the odds weren't very
good for me making it to medical school.

Chemistry and I were not getting along very well
and by the last six weeks of the term, I knew I was in
trouble. With fear and trembling, I made an
appointment with the professor, a harsh and
extremely impersonal man who seemed to be about
half ticked-off most of the time. But knowing that I
needed some help and in hopes of getting some
guidance and direction to bring my grade up from an
F to maybe an F+, I sucked it up and went to see

him. Big mistake.

After a few minutes of conversation with him, during which time he looked over my test papers and grades, he made a startling statement. "Young man, the problem is, you're not college material. The best and wisest thing you could do would be to drop out of school and get a job. That way, you'd stop wasting my time and your money." Wow! Was that a kick in the teeth or what?! I had been in college two months, had just turned 18, and was being told it was a mistake and I needed to quit! My plans had included college from the time I was in Juanita Long's sixth grade class. And after eight weeks, I was being told by a professor to give it up and quit! Not hardly.

Even though I was in trouble in chemistry, (and eventually took the flag) I wasn't ready to pack it in and head to the house. Forty-five years later, (in hopes that an honest confession will be good for the soul) I'm now ready to get real with you. When I earned my second doctorate, I had a fantasy of walking into his office in full cap, gown, and hood and reminding him of his careless and reckless conduct with me as an 18-year-old college freshman many years before. In my fantasy, I could hear myself saying, "How do you like me now?" Then I would stand straight and tall and wait to see what that old coot would say. Pretty tacky of me, huh? Well, I've been known to do some tacky things for real— at least this one was only a fantasy.

When I've told this story in the past, some people

immediately assume that his stunning remarks were done deliberately to motivate me and that I'm leading up to saying his input served as a catalyst to make me try harder. Wrong, on both accounts. Nothing about his input was helpful. Truth be told, it was devastating and his remarks tremendously weakened my already flimsy self-confidence. It would take years to remove the dagger of doubt so carelessly flung by a cantankerous, ill-tempered, professor.

Interestingly enough, (which I didn't put together until many years later) that teacher was in the last phase of his teaching career and in all likelihood saw himself as a failure. He was nearing retirement, yet the only classes he was allowed to teach were freshmen courses. Isn't it funny how our own internal issues of self-doubt and feelings of failure get dumped into the laps of others. Well no, it isn't funny– it's tragic– yep, tragic– that's what it is.

Back to the doctors in Parsons. Dr. L.E. Luna was wonderfully helpful to our community. For example, he gave the football team their annual physicals for free. And even though he wasn't our regular doctor, he was extremely nice to my family and me. Before stitching up a huge gash in my arm which resulted from a serious bicycle wreck, he carefully picked out the gravel with tweezers and talked to me with calm assurance to keep me from having a seizure! He loved hunting and fishing, called all the boys *Rooster*, and was a great encourager and supporter and I loved him dearly, which you'll understand when you read on.

Since we had no junior high football team, with special permission, some of the 7th and 8th grade boys were allowed to be on the high school team. When I was in the 8th grade, I got to play in one high school football game for a few plays. The following week, I received a note on letterhead paper from Dr. Luna:

"Dear Donnis,   I saw you get into Friday night's football game. You looked good and made a great block on that big fellow coming down field. In fact, I saw you block him twice! Keep up the good work. Just wanted you to know that somebody was watching."

Can you imagine how such a letter from such a man, impacted a 100 pound twelve year old boy playing in his first football game?! If not, let me sit down with you sometime, and in perhaps an hour I can get the point across.

➤

Sports and More Sports

All of us who wear the title *Southerner* know without question that athletics in the South is a religion. It was no different in our little county. Even though we seldom had outstanding teams in any sport, it was still taken very seriously. Few things draw small communities together like athletics and during the 50's, for boys, be it right or wrong, playing team sports was almost considered a rite of passage.

Being a little short on entertainment meant large crowds came to Little League and Babe Ruth League baseball games. Those teams were coached by people like Kinky Lancaster, Henry Evans, Keylon Barrett, Royce Reynolds, Hugh Carrington, Earl West, Lamarse Brasher, James Arnold, and Lewis Harrell, and many others. For a few years, my father, Maxie Doyle, was in charge of the concession stand and maintenance of the baseball field.

All of those men, along with many others and numerous women, put in countless hours to bring organized baseball to Decatur County in 1954. We had real uniforms made by our own local garment factory, Salant and Salant. They were bonafide baseball uniforms made of flannel with baggy legs and team names on the front and numbers on the back.

The four Little League teams were the Cardinals, Red Sox, Giants, and Yankees. Coached by Kinky Lancaster and James Arnold, I played for the Yankees. Ray West, who lived down the street from me, coached one of the other teams. As a pitcher, he had been in the St. Louis Cardinals organization and he spent countless hours teaching me how to pitch.

It is my guess that those of us who played Little League baseball during that first season count that as one of the most cherished childhood memories. It certainly is for me.

Just for the record, in case you're ever on *Jeopardy*, I hit the first-ever over the fence home run in the history of Decatur County Little League! (Yes, on occasions, I still autograph baseballs. So, send them along and I'll be glad to accommodate you– for a small fee of course!)

The Yankees
Decatur County Little League– 1954
Coaches– James Arnold and Kinky Lancaster

Front L-R– Jimmy Lynn Walker, Doug Vice, Jimmy Monroe, Jimmy Jones, Doug McCormick.

Back L-R– Don Doyle, Jerry Wallace, Louie Lacey, Fred Ward, Jordan Moore, Jerry Paul Teague, Reed Paterson

The following year they added Babe Ruth Baseball which was for 13, 14, and 15 year olds. Thus, some of us were able to play organized baseball from age 12 through 15.

With four teams in the Babe Ruth League– Braves, Indians, Tigers, Dodgers– a lot of kids in Decatur County were fortunate enough to put in many hours during the summertime playing baseball. Equally as many adults spent as many hours making the program work successfully– coaches, umpires, scorekeepers, announcers, concession workers, and those who maintained the fields– all were volunteers and all seemed to enjoy the contribution they were making.

One of my vivid memories of those years of youth baseball was the large number of people who attended. The bleachers were always filled with family, friends, fans, and folks from all over the county who cheered and yelled their heads off for their favorite teams and players.

The Braves
Decatur County Babe Ruth League– 1956
Coach– Lamarse Brasher

Front Row L-R: Bill Scallions, Jerry Paul Teague, Buddy Tuten, Bill Martin, Lamarse Brasher, Don Doyle, Butch McClure, K.O. Hays Back Row L-R– Steve Young, Chet Gordon, Ted Funderburk, Sam McIllwain, Bobby Adams, Arthur Ray Montgomery, Joe Reynolds.

➤

In 1955, John and Nancy Tucker, along with Pete and Betty Riggins, came to Parsons. John was named head football and baseball coach at PHS and Pete was hired as head basketball coach for both the boys and girls and assistant football coach. Tucker was only twenty-one years old when he came to mentor the Parsons High School Tigers. He was quite simply the most knowledgeable football coach I ever played for and very likely the most brilliant who's ever coached in the county, even to the present day.

John Tucker was from Jackson and for more than four decades was one of the most successful high school coaches in Tennessee and the entire country. Most of his career was spent as head coach at Milan High School, then later Humboldt High.

In the year he coached in Parsons, it was obvious he was incredibly gifted in the wisdom of the game. In looking back on it (and I'm sure he would agree), he was equally immature. He had a lot to teach but he was inexperienced in how to handle and lead teenagers. Half the team quit before the end of the first week of practice. As a result, we only dressed out 14-18 players and that included freshmen like me. At 5'7" and 125 pounds, I was the second string quarterback and even played in a few games. My playing time came when starter, Bob Herndon, one of my closest friends, would get hurt. I remember feeling more than a little uneasy when I would be sent in at the same moment Bobby was being carried out!

Given the fact that this man was only in my life for one school year and it occurred almost 50 years ago, it is amazing how many things I remember about Coach Tucker. Some of his platitudes were:

"We're not gonna stop practice until somebody bleeds."
"If you stay on this team, you're gonna have pride in wearing the red jersey."
"Never take off your headgear– never."
"If you ever go down on more than one knee, you better be unconscious."
"We may not win, but we're always gonna look like winners– always."

When he first arrived in Parsons, he found out I played football and had a lawn mower, so, he recruited me and my lawn mower and we, along with some others, cut the grass on the football field. He once took me to Jackson where I met his family at the Tucker Motel, located in Hickville at the corner of Tucker St. and N. Highland, which was owned by his father, Mike Tucker. When he introduced me to his sister, Michael Ann, he said, "If you ever make a pass at her, I'll kill you." Well, at age thirteen, the only pass I really knew about was with a football, but after his warning, I knew I'd never throw it to his sister!

He was a nut about football, almost as much as me, and when he found out I had a Foto Football set (an old-time version of board game football), he wanted to play. We played a lot, then he borrowed the set so he could play by himself, or with whomever he could engage. He kept that set for the rest of the year. In fact, I'm not sure I ever got it back.

John Tucker hated basketball almost as much as he loved football. For example, to show his disdain for basketball, one of his favorite pastimes was to stand at half court and try to bank a football off the backboard for a basket which infuriated Coach Riggins. But the weird part was he could make about a third of his throws.

He annoyed Coach Riggins even more when he announced that football practice for all backs and receivers would start the Monday after the last game of the season. In a small high school, it was the norm for several football players to also play basketball but football ended just as basketball season was beginning. Tucker didn't say we couldn't play basketball, he just said, "If you want to play football next season, practice will begin Monday." We got the point, and Coach Riggins got the shaft.

Coach Tucker organized a football club that had a rather bizarre initiation ritual. In order to become a member of the football club, the guys had to wear a dress to school and carry a raw egg in the ankle of their socks. Of course, within no time at all, those eggs were quickly broken and we spent the remainder of the day squishing with socks full of raw eggs. He raised enough money from merchants to buy everyone on the team a letter jacket, which was a first for Parsons High School, and man did we ever wear those jackets with pride.

During his one and only season in Parsons, we won three games, tied one, and lost six. One of those losses was to Decaturville, our county arch rival who had not beaten Parsons in twenty-five years or at least that's the way I remember it.

Decaturville was loaded that year and a heavy

favorite. John Tucker was mortified that he might be the first Parsons coach in a quarter century to lose to them, so he did everything imaginable to offset the odds. He made up a dummy football player with the number of their ace tailback, Jerry Brasher, number 65, and hung it in effigy in the gym.   Then on Wednesday night before our pep rally on Thursday, he snuck in and stole the dummy and blamed it on Decaturville. To this day, he denies that he did it. But if he didn't, I'm positive he was responsible for having it done! That was supposed to make us fighting mad. Prior to that happening on Wednesday night, he had held a full-scale practice in a pouring rain with some places on the field standing in water. And it was cold. Not only did the stealing of the dummy not fire us up but practicing in the cold rain made half the team sick. We lost 7-0.

One of our key players was a kid from Linden, named Gerald Zemer. He was huge, at least for those days. Stood about 6'3" and weighed 235 lbs. And he was as strong as an ox. One day, he lifted the back of coach Tucker's Studebaker pickup by himself and someone placed a coke case on the inside of each wheel. When coach tried to drive away, the back tires wouldn't touch the ground and he just sat and spun until a couple of guys pushed him off the blocks. Gerald Zemer was a great guy, but he had never played football in his life. As I remember it, the first game he ever saw, he played in.

During the season, Coach Tucker discovered that

Zemer could kick the daylights out of a football off the kicking tee. So, we practiced with him kicking off. At the next game, we lost the coin toss and they elected to receive. Zemer was on. The team lined up and he was in position and everything looked good. We could just see that ball going through the back of the end zone. One problem. Coach had forgotten to tell Zemer that he had to wait for the referee to blow the whistle to start the game. When Gerald was ready he started running toward the ball. That's when the referee blew the whistle. When Zemer heard it, he was about two strides from the ball, so he stopped. Coach yelled "kick it," so he took a half step and pooched the ball about ten yards down field. I cannot remember exactly what Coach Tucker said, but I'm pretty sure it had something to do with Zemer's family heritage.

One game that stands out in my memory was Camden. We went down crooked highway 69 to play an undefeated team that was loaded. Early in the second quarter, Bob Herndon, our fine quarterback got hurt. As the backup quarterback, Coach Tucker yelled my name, got in my face and told me what plays to call on the first two snaps and gave me emphatic instructions to "hand the ball off to Thomas King, Gaylon Yates, or Thomas Hayes and don't fumble the ball! Do you understand me?" "Yes sir, you can count on me, sir!" I said shaking in my boots or rather my cleats.

On the first play, I handed off to Gaylon Yates

running off tackle and it went pretty well. Feeling a little confidence, I was ready for the second play, which was called Quick 38 and was a swift pitchout to fullback Thomas King going wide right. I missed him by about three feet which, of course, was the equivalent of that dreaded fumble! But, the Lord God himself was on my side because I did recover the ball which is the only thing that kept me from having to make a trip to the local hospital to remove coach's brogan from my rear end. It was also on that play that I was officially introduced to #14, Camden's middle linebacker, a kid whose name I still remember but will not disclose. Lining up right over our center, Norris Douglas, he looked me square in the eye and on every play talked trash. Even though I couldn't understand much of what he was saying, I could clearly see that he was snaggle-toothed with tobacco juice running down his chin. Many years later, it was rumored that he had a small role in *Deliverance.* (Just kidding).

In spite of getting hit several times by "old nasty mouth", I didn't fumble again but we lost 35-0. Even though I had a few bruises from being hit by #14, the thing that bruised my ego the most came from Coach Tucker. I was hyped up about having played so much and he was mad because we had lost so badly.

On the bus ride back home, over horribly crooked Highway 69, he told everyone to put their heads down and keep their mouths shut. As usual, I was sitting right behind him because I always wanted to be as close as possible to devour every morsel of football information and knowledge that he would dish out. Since I was always more than a little chatty, after a few minutes, I impulsively said something to Bob Herndon sitting next to me who was still hurting from his injury. Tucker whirled around and said, "I said keep your mouth shut, Doyle!" and he slapped me on top of the head. Embarrassed and with my feelings hurt more than my head, I put my head back down and didn't say another word. And that, dear heart, is "the way we were" in the 50's.

The most indelible memory I have of Coach John Tucker came during baseball season. He was head baseball coach, too, and I was the starting second baseman. In a game with Henderson, we were behind by one run and I was on third base. Tucker was the third base coach and said to me, "Doyle, if that ball is hit to the right side, you better score."

That was standard baseball strategy and I knew it. Well, the next batter hit a ground ball toward second and I broke for the plate but I lost my footing and slipped a little and immediately retreated to third. Tucker was livid and went into one of his tirades.

"What in the hell do you think you're doing?" he bellowed.

"I didn't think I could make it, Coach," I replied.

"Who's paying you to THINK? Damn you, if that run costs us the game, you'll flunk P.E."

Well, it did. And he did. We lost the game by one run and he gave me a D in P.E. for that grading period. As a result, I was ineligible for the Beta Club which required a 92 overall average and no grade below C. It was the only D on my freshman report card and I still had above a 92 average. Nevertheless, I was denied membership into the Beta Club.

Thinking back on it, I'm sure Coach Tucker had no idea the impact of giving me that D. It was just his way of making a point about following instructions. I'm equally sure if I had talked to him about it, he would have changed the grade. Or if my parents had talked to him, I think he would have made the adjustment. But in that era, at that point in my life, confronting a teacher personally or asking my parents to intervene on my behalf was not even a consideration. That's just the way it was for me, at least, during the 50's.

Without a doubt, I learned more football from John Tucker than all the other coaches I ever played for combined. My guess is everybody on that team would say the same thing. As a result, two years later we had a championship season as a direct result (I believe) of his coaching.

One of our team members, Donald "Duck" Dickson, was a terrific athlete with a lot of raw talent. He was such a hard hitter that he got a concussion about twice a game, even wearing those marvelously ugly, leather, Notre Dame helmets that Coach Tucker had acquired. If in those days a player had to miss a game after a concussion, Duck wouldn't have played but half a season! He went on to be a star player at Ole Miss, and I always believed that the year he played for John Tucker probably did more to get him a scholarship than anything else.

Coach Tucker intensified my love for the game by the knowledge he transferred. He taught me a lot about discipline, commitment, and hard work, and for that I will be forever grateful. Thinking back on those experiences, my biggest regrets are that he didn't stay in Parsons to coach for the next few years and that I didn't kick his butt for slapping me and giving me that D in P.E. (Just kidding– I think.)

As was stated earlier, two years after John Tucker left Parsons, under Coach Jack Southerland, our '57 football team was the best to come out of PHS for many years before and equally as many after. It was a memorable season to be sure; one that none of us who played will ever forget. Just reminiscing about it brings back distinct memories of the sights (particularly the cheerleaders), the sounds (from proud town folks), and the smells (specifically of sweaty uniforms, analgesic balm, and "tough skin.")

Our opening game was at home against a very fine Selmer team. The thing I remember most about that game happened on the sideline. Taking a pitchout, Bobby Herndon went wide left and with a great block from Donald "Duck" Dickson went ninety yards for a touchdown.

Red Gilbreath, an avid supporter, whose son, Roger, was on our team, was helping carry the chains (as he always did) which meant he was practically on the field of play. Red owned the Western Auto Store and although he was only in his early 40's, he seemed like an old man to us; a likable old man, I might add.

Bobby broke free down the left side line and was tight roping the chalk. Holding the chain stick at the fifteen, Red saw him coming and knew what was about to happen– Bobby Herndon was in the clear with nothing but real estate between him and pay dirt. That's when baldheaded, forty-year-old Red Gilbreath did the unthinkable. Without a trace of foresight that he would undergo unmerciful teasing and embarrassment, or possible consequences that very likely would keep him bedridden for a solid week, impulsively threw down the chain stick and started running. By the time Bobby caught up to him at the twenty-five, Red was at full throttle and ran seventy-five yards stride for stride with Bobby Herndon, an eighteen-year-old phenom and the fastest player on our team.

As the quarterback and pitch man to Bobby, I followed behind down field and saw the whole thing unfold. Bobby, running at full speed, Red right beside

him yelling to the top of his lungs for seventy-five yards, "RUN, BOBBY, RUN!" In my mind's memory bank, I can see it as clearly right now as I did then. I don't even have to close my eyes.

Our team went 8-2 and was invited to have a rematch with Huntingdon in the Exchange Bowl in Jackson, an honor never before afforded a PHS team. Huntingdon had beaten us 21-0 in the regular season on a frozen field, a game in which I got my hand broken. A fellow named Warren Blankenship (who went on to play for the Tennessee Vols) with forethought and malice of doing bodily harm, stepped squarely on top of my left hand and broke several bones, which I thought was kinda tacky. Although I loved the game, I wasn't a very good football player–too small to start with and I made up for by also being slow! The next day when Dr. Hubert Conger put my hand in a cast, I pretty well concluded that my future after high school would not include playing football.

So, when the proposal for a rematch with the Mustangs from Huntingdon came up, I still had a sore hand and a vivid memory of what that redneck, tough guy had done to me, and the possibility of getting some overdue revenge by playing them again was all I'd been waiting for!! (If you believe that, I've got some ocean front property in Arizona that I'd like to show you!)

Truth be told, I'd had my fill of the Huntingdon Mustangs, so, when the team was asked to vote on playing the rematch, I voiced my opinion that I'd be open to at least considering another offer! I was out voted and we were beaten the second time 25-6. At least, I didn't get my hand broken in that game. I don't think I played any better, I just did a better job of staying out of the way of Mr. Blankenship.

Actually, we might have fared better the second time around if it hadn't been for the Asian flu bug. Our team was hit hard and so many were sick that the game had to be postponed and rescheduled. To say the least, we weren't at full strength but I suspect the outcome would have been about the same, Asian flu bug or not. Back to more pleasant memories.

The most memorable game of that stellar '57

football season, was the victory over Lexington for the first time in anybody's memory. Without question, it was one of the highlights of my high school days. Final score– Parsons 40– Lexington 0.

The Lexington game was always the last of the season. Normally, they put a pretty bad whupping on us. And I promise you, that every person who was at that game can still remember that 40 to zip victory in 1957– at least the players for sure.

While that may have been the biggest athletic victory in many years, the biggest athletic upset by a Parsons team in the 50's came a few months earlier during basketball season.

Beech Bluff was a small school in Madison County that had a great basketball tradition and had beaten us earlier in the year in our gym by more than fifty points. They broke the 100 mark which was nearly unheard of in high school basketball during that era. Their coach had been unmerciful and kept his starters in the entire game and embarrassed our team, our fans, and our coach, Mr. Jack Southerland.

Mr. Jack had buried his mother earlier in the day and then came to coach our team and was humiliated. After the game, he confronted the Beech Bluff coach about running up the score. The opposing coach indignantly replied, "If you've got the horses, you let em run!" Mr. Jack responded, "That's fine. But I promise you, it'll come back to you."

Beech Bluff finished the regular season with a perfect 30-0 record. Entering the first round of the district tournament, they were heavy favorites to win it all, including the state tournament in Nashville. Supporters had even bought new jackets for them to wear through the tournaments. But "A funny thing happened on the way to Music City."

In the first game of the district tournament, they were derailed by the low ranking, unpretentious, Parsons High School Tigers– 53-52!

Mr. Jack wasn't a man to boast, but after the game, when he shook hands with the Beech Bluff coach, he said, "Do you still think it's a good idea to let the horses run?"

Parsons businessman and civic leader, Doug Hayes, was so excited that he treated the entire team to a steak dinner in Jackson. That was especially good for me since I didn't play much and riding the pine can make a young boy mighty hungry!

More Memorabilia & Stuff

In the 50's, anything made in Japan was ridiculed and called cheap. Long since forgotten cars were still being made and sold: Packard, Hudson, Kaiser, Frazier, and Willys. My first car was a 1952 Willys sedan that cost me $200.00 which I paid for with my paper route earnings. Every Friday afternoon I made a payment at the Farmers Bank until I had satisfied the loan. Then, of course, I was ready for something cooler, so, I traded in the great little Willys sedan for a black, 2 door, V-8, '51 Ford– exactly like the one used in the very popular movie, *Thunder Road*. Trading in my Willys, I paid the car lot in Lexington $175.00 to boot and had my new old car. Big mistake! It was a piece of junk, but it was cool, and that was of the utmost importance in those days.

During that era, you could actually buy a Henry J (named after Henry J. Kaiser) through Sears and Roebuck's mail order catalog. In Parsons you could buy a Packard or a Studebaker from Long Equipment Co., Goff Motor Company sold Fords, and Townsend Chevrolet handled the Chevys.

Cars did not have seat belts and what few babies rode in car seats were not strapped in. Power steering and power brakes were new. Few had them. The only power steering we had was a steering wheel knob. The Edsel came and went and the only foreign car any of us had ever seen was a VW Beetle, which we thought looked pretty stupid. Little did we know... .

There was no such thing as styrofoam cups or velcro. We read about velcro in Reader's Digest (the student edition, of course) but it was much later before it actually hit the market, at least in Parsons.

Nothing came in plastic bottles. Cokes came in thick glass bottles. The only beverage that came in a can was beer. It took a "church key" to open it. Wrist watches had to be wound regularly and the value of them was based on the number of jewels inside, not outside. The Elgin and Bulova companies made 17, 19, 21, and even 23 jewel watches; the more jewels, the more expensive, but again, we're talking about the jewels inside, not outside.

Friday night was fight night. That's when boxing matches were telecast– Jersey Joe Walcott, Rocky Marciano, Ezzard Charles, Sugar Ray Robinson, Ingemar Johannson, Gene Fulmer, Carmen Basilio– those were a few of the best fighters. Sponsored by Gillette, I can hear the announcer now: "The Gillette Cavalcade of Sports is on the air." Then the Gillette singers would chime in, To look sharp every time you shave, to feel sharp and be on the ball, just be sharp with Gillette blue blades, the very best and closest shave of all.

On Saturday nights we watched Lucky Strike's *Your Hit Parade* with regular singers: Snooky Lanson, Dorothy Collins, Johnny Desmond, and Giselle MacKenzie. Television was black and white and it took a long time for the tubes to warm up after you turned it on. The screens were very small with snowy pictures but we were fascinated by *Ozzie and Harriett*, *Toast of the Town with Ed Sullivan*, *The Red Skelton Show*, *Sid Caesar and Imogene Coco*, *Father*

Knows Best, I Love Lucy, My Little Margie, The Trouble with Father (Stu Erwin) *Our Miss Brooks,* (Eve Arden) and *The $64,000 Question* (hosted by Hal March.)

Former major leaguer, Chuck Conners, starred in *The Rifleman,* and Richard Boone was a respectable bounty hunter in *Have Gun, Will Travel.* A hot new western television program was called *Rawhide.* The trail boss was Gil Favor (Mr. Favor to the cowpokes) whose sidekick was a young man named *Rowdy Yates* who was destined for Hollywood stardom. Can you name him? That's right, it was Clint Eastwood.

Still speaking of television– on Saturday night we had a regular dose of Billy Graham's, *Hour of Decision,* "...foah eveah, and eveah... I'm asking you to get up out of youah seat, right now... foah eveah and eveah... amen."

Stories from Parsons High School

Bertie Dailey was our principal; Hugh Houston gave us a good dose of Science, Biology, Chemistry, and Physics. (Can you imagine anyone today teaching all those courses?!) Hilda Welch gave us a steady and solid diet of English literature. Ruth Carrington taught us all how to type– which incidently was the most important course I took in high school. (I wish I had told her that.) Everett McIllwain taught an untold number of boys about agriculture and shop; Barbara Bowman "shushed" us all in the library. Miss Barbara lived with her brother, Mr. Albert. Neither of

them ever married and were just two of the finest
people that the good Lord ever made. Humm, I
wonder if there's a connection between being
unmarried and a nice person? Probably not... .

Speaking of Miss Barbara. In those days, one of
the practical jokes boys loved involved rattlesnake
rattlers. Pay attention now and I'll tell you how it was
done. First, you take a hair pin (a Bobbie pin as some
people called them), spread it wide and bend the ends
down about a quarter of an inch. Then you take a
small rubber band and run it through one of the holes
in a large button. Next you loop the rubber band
over the hair pin and twist it until it's wound very
tight. Then you place it in a small envelope, holding
it firmly so the button and rubber band won't come
unwound. You tell your victim you killed a six foot
rattlesnake and kept the rattlers. "Actually, they're in
this envelope," you say, handing the envelope to your
guinea pig. When the envelope is opened, the rubber
band rapidly unwinds, the button flies round and
round and sounds exactly like a rattlesnake. There's
not a person alive who won't scream, jump, squeal or
worse! (I'm sure you get the picture.)

Now back to our librarian, Barbara Bowman. Are
you way ahead of me? You guessed it, I played the
rattlesnake rattlers trick on her. She was about half
asleep at the time but I can promise you she had no
trouble staying awake the rest of the day. I'll also
swear on a stack of Bibles ten feet high, that I had no
intention of scaring that woman within an inch of her

death. My goal was to just rouse her up a bit from the boredom of being a high school librarian and sitting there all day "schushing" hormone enraged teenagers. So, you see, my intentions were of high moral fiber, and in my mind, I was doing this dear lady a favor by adding some spice to her otherwise dreadfully boring day job. Yeah, right, I can hear you saying! And you're right again, it didn't quite work out that way.

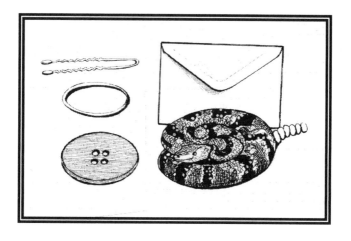

Miss Barbara screamed so loud that everyone in the library jumped off their seats. I jumped about three feet high myself. Do you understand what I'm saying, this woman SCREAMED. I just knew she was going to have a heart attack. They heard it all the way down the hall to the principal's office. At that very moment, I assure you, I was wishing I had bypassed Miss Barbara with my little trick and long before Tanya Tucker recorded it, I was thinking "It's a little too late to do the right thing now!"

In a matter of seconds, Mr. Bertie Dailey, our principal, came running into the library, which was the only time I ever saw him run during my entire years of high school. To say the least, he was a portly man who wore his pants substantially above his belly button and you could just look at him and know that he wasn't a man who ran wind sprints, not now nor ever before. But he was definitely in a fast paced trot when he showed up in the library.

Seeing all of it unfold, my entire life flashed in front of my eyes and I thought my goose was cooked and I was pretty sure my school days were over. Fact is, I was already wondering how I was going to like factory work. My father had worked at the factory most of his adult life, so I figured I could adjust to it. It crossed my mind that it was time for me to start collecting my personals and head to the house.

Surprise, shock, shezam! When Mr. Dailey heard the story, he started to chuckle in that unique way that he laughed. He laughed from way back in his throat, sort of a "hea, hea, hea" and that portly belly would jiggle, which was below his big black belt that was buckled several inches above the belly button. I had seen it many times (the laugh, that is) but never was I so pleased to hear him laugh and see his belly jiggle as that day. Then Miss Barbara got to laughing. Not wanting to be a party pooper, I quickly joined in!

As Mr. Dailey turned to leave, he glanced at me over the rim of his glasses, "Son, I don't think I'd do that again!" he said in a pretty feeble but commendable effort at sounding serious, obviously still holding back another chuckle.

"No sir, you can count on it," I said, relieved that the factory had just lost a good young worker.

Shortly thereafter, Miss Barbara left for the teacher's lounge, perhaps to rearrange her garments or possibly change some!

➤

Not all of my high school activity involved getting in trouble with people like Miss Barbara Bowman. Like most other students in small high schools, I was involved in many activities. Played football, baseball, and basketball; a member of the cast in both the junior and senior class plays; and I was honored by being voted as one of the class favorites and chosen by the student body as MR PHS. Reflecting back on those experiences brings up another memory which shows just how culturally and socially out of touch I was during those years. Some folks would argue that I haven't improved much but I would maintain that even though I may not show it, at least now I know better. In fact, at that 40th reunion, more than one person said to me, "You haven't changed a bit" which I'm not sure was a compliment! Anyway, back to my story of social and cultural ineptness.

Being elected MR PHS meant, along with MISS PHS, Bonny Blankenship, we would appear in the yearbook, *The '59 Tiger*. As the lead picture for the Class Favorites section, editor, Sarah Gordon, wanted these pictures to be "formal." So, Bonny would wear an evening gown and I would wear comparable attire. To go with my one pair of dark dress pants, I borrowed a white dinner jacket, bought a bow tie from *Palmer and Adair* (which would later become *Zula's Family Fashions*, my mother's store) and got all spiffied up for the photo shoot. Touching up the flattop with the butch wax, I hit the underarms with a little deodorant, and splashed on a hefty round of Ole Spice. All that was left was slipping on some shoes and I was ready for the man with the camera.

Looking in my closet revealed the only shoes I had were athletic shoes and some black and white saddle oxfords that had been my trademark for all of my senior year. Those black and white oxfords were my school shoes, church shoes, and any other occasion shoes. Choosing between baseball spikes, football cleats, Chuck Taylor Converse All-Star basketball shoes or my all-purpose black and whites, meant the oxfords got the call. So, that's what I wore to the photo session– white jacket, black pants, black bow tie, white socks, and black and white saddle oxfords.

The year book of 1959 has it recorded for eternity, MISS PHS descending the staircase in Raymond and Sophia Townsend's house and me with outstretched arms, greeting her with white dinner jacket, black trousers, black bow tie and **black and white saddle oxfords.** The best or worst part of that story is that I didn't know there was anything wrong with that combination and apparently neither did anyone else or perhaps they were just too shocked to mention it!

Remembering the Parsons High School Class of 1959

Leeburn Harris and Edward Hearington were the teachers who served as sponsors for our senior class. They did a great job in giving us guidance and direction, especially in making arrangements for our senior trip. Leeburn Harris was the band director, taught some classes and even directed our senior play. He was also a major influence in talking me into attending Memphis State University and even went with Olis Quinn and me to look over the campus and to take the entrance exam. For all of that, I will be forever grateful.

As I reflect on those fifty high school seniors from the Parsons High School class of 1959, I hope every reader will remember some of your classmates with the same fondness and affection that I feel for mine and I strongly suspect that you will.

Suggestion: Take a pad of paper and write down all those you remember from your senior class and then write a sentence or paragraph about each person. You will be surprised at how much you remember, how many times you will smile, and how good it feels to reminisce. If you get stumped, dig out that old year book that's tucked away in moth balls or in an old cedar chest and thumb through your book of memories. Better yet, find someone with whom you can share those memories– a spouse, good friend, one of your own children if you can get them to agree to it, or best of all, an old classmate. It'll do you good. I promise.

PARSONS HIGH SCHOOL
CLASS and FACULTY
1959

CLASSMATES

To talk about my class mates has to begin with recognition of "The Baker's Dozen"– those thirteen who went through all twelve grades together. Bonny Blankenship, Gerald Dickson, Sara Gibson, Martha Kay Houston, David Hayes, Joyce Jordan, Charlotte Lackey, Sammy McIllwain, Bobby Myracle, Titus Shelby, Diane Tinker, Marijon Young, and the author. What a treat to have that many friends who puttered along together through all twelve grades. To each of them, I say– "Saluutte!" Now, in no particular order, let me tell you about our entire class.

➤

Diane Tinker had a great hook shot and her two-toned yellow and white 1957 Ford station wagon carried many of us to a lot of places. She was one of the solid class leaders who influenced us all. *Sara Gibson* was the consummate cheerleader and served in that capacity for all four years of high school. *John Townsend* rode a Cushman scooter forever until he got his driver's license and a '57 Chevy.

Olis Quinn Jr., will always be everybody's "Teddy Bear" and kept us in tears of laughter. No surprise that he was voted Most Courteous Boy! I'll always appreciate that he and I went to Memphis State University together and were roommates for a while.

Class President, *Sammy McIllwain*, kept us "responsible" by his sterling example. He was a fine athlete and was a vital part of our football team for all four years and was voted Most Athletic Boy.

Anita Milam's academic brilliance made us all feel

inferior because we were no match for her. Nor was
anybody else. But she always worked hard not to
flaunt it or even call attention to it. There was never
any doubt she'd be Valedictorian– she was.

Bobby Myracle was everybody's "Monk" and a
friend to everyone who knew him. Class Vice
President, *Jerry Wallace*, elevated "easy going" to a
new level and along with being football captain was
also named Best All-Around, Best Looking, and the
F.H.A. Beau– how's that for a great combination.

Michael Jordan set the example for us with good
manners, proper etiquette, and the right decorum.
Martha Kay Houston was mature and classy and
showed a refinement regarding how to dress and how
to act, which I, for one, needed.

All of us knew *Linda Graves, Bonny Blankenship*,
and *Patsy Mooney*– the Gold Dust Trio– were just
three of the nicest people you'd ever meet or want to
meet. *Linda Graves* had a great smile, wonderful
laugh, and great life view and was a treat for us all. In
addition to being Miss PHS, *Bonny Blankenship* was
the F.F.A. Sweetheart and also tied for Most Popular
Girl along with *Patsy Mooney* who had moved to
Parsons from Memphis and fit into our group like a
glove fits a hand.

Titus Ray Shelby showed great loyalty and respect
for his friends and was voted *Mostly Likely to Succeed*,
and did. That's when he immediately became T.R.
Shelby. He got rid of Titus about as quickly as I did
my first name. With my given name being Donnis, it

was quite simple just to shorten it to Don. Tit-us didn't have that option!

T.R. shared the Most Likely to Succeed title with *Odis Haggard.* Years later, when Merle Haggard came on the music scene, I thought maybe Odis had changed his name, too! Or perhaps *Reuben (Haggard.)*

Linda Livingston was selected as the Daughters of American Revolution representative and *The Girl Most Likely to Succeed.* We never doubted she would. She did. With a head full of curly hair, *John Tom Clifft* had a smile as big as Texas and a well balanced personality.

Kay Reynolds was unusually attractive and full of school spirit. *Marijon Young* was a great friend to everybody, full of fun, had a great laugh, loved PHS and still does.

Charlotte Lackey always had a great sense of humor and a steady boyfriend. So did *Freda Gurley*, who was voted Best Looking. *Margie Perry* kept us laughing.

Along with being voted Most Intellectual, *Jo Ethel Forsha* was a fine basketball player. She and *Brenda Taylor* were busy shooting baskets and being who they were, nice friendly girls. *Claudean Inman* had her eye on Cleo Rhodes forever. What a great match.

Class officer, *Joyce Jordan*, had the prettiest smile you ever saw and had more friends than you could count. Joining our class in tenth grade, *Nancy Yarbro* was a good addition to our bunch.

Joe Houston was solid as a rock and with a cotton-top head of hair always will be "Frosty." *Jimmie Ann*

Long took part in nearly everything, was everybody's friend, and was chosen Miss Home Economics.

Even though, he was the youngest member of our class, none of us were surprised that *Bunis Smith* was voted Most Intellectual and became a minister. *David Hayes* was... well, what can I say, just David.

Tom Bawcum could blow the heck out of a horn, played football and basketball, and spent more than his fair share of time nursing a pinball machine. The class of '58's loss was definitely our gain when *Sandra Hayes* came back to graduate with us after saying "I do" to Thomas Carrington.

We knew *Robert Canada* would be successful at something; just weren't sure what. But we never dreamed he'd coach golf at Oral Roberts University, where rumor had it that his biggest dilemma was keeping the holes on the greens from "healing up." (Forgive me for being so tacky.)

Larry Watson, (coach called him " Lefthander") was the best pure shooter of a basketball that PHS ever had. In another setting, he'd have played at the next level. If they had given an "oscar" for jumping ability, *Oscar Spence* would have won an "oscar." He could leap like a gazelle and was one of the nicest guys you ever met. On the basketball court, teaming up with Big *Bill Colwick*, they were hard to beat inside.

Five Korean war vets came back to school on the GI bill and finished with us. *Randolph Higdon, Charles Lyles, James Price, Billy Mays,* and *Clois Maness* added much maturity to our young and naive lives.

Everybody knew Salutatorian, *Sarah Gordon,* would be a doctor– we just didn't know what kind. Sure wish she was my Pharmacy Doc. *Becky Holt* was voted Best All-Around Girl– no surprise she became a superb school teacher. What a sweetheart. Enough so, that she was voted Homecoming Queen. For me, and I suspect Jerry Wallace, too, the best part of being the football captain was kissing the queen!

(From left– Jerry Wallace, Becky Holt, and yours truly!)

➢

At the present, (August, 2004) over fifteen percent of our '59 graduating classmates are deceased. Nine out of the fifty died much too early: *Randolph Higdon*, one of those vets who really fit into our class, nice person; *David "Facts" Hayes*, a wheeler/dealer who was always making a deal; *Bill "Highpockets" Colwick* was his own young man who bleached his hair in front before it was cool, and was totally unembarrassed to loudly sing his favorite songs; *Tyrone Kirby* was non-assuming and quiet, yet he wore ducktails before it was cool, at least in Parsons; *Tommy Harris* was a great guy— friendly, smart, likable— who dedicated his professional life to being a college professor; *Donald "Popcorn" Moore* was the working man's young man— got the nickname from working at the Rustic Theater; *Rev. Bunis Smith*, one of the nicest guys you'd ever meet, died much too early; *Gerald Dickson* was a solid guy, who could "Bile them cabbage down," and if you were going to war, he's the guy you'd want to go with you. He did. It shortened his life.

In those days, if you looked in Webster's under "cheerleader" there should have been a picture of *Kay Reynolds*. At our 30th reunion in 1989, Kay whispered, "I need to come talk to you." I gave her a business card and said, "Give me a call." She never called. A few days later, in the presence of her mother, an estranged husband shot her to death, then himself. She shouldn't have died that way. It still haunts me.

➤

The Parsons High School class of 1959 was a group of typical kids from a small town in the rural South. Just like those before us and those after us, we had our hopes and dreams as we sang "Now is the Hour" at the commencement ceremony. But in many ways our class was quite atypical of those that came before us and those that came after. There was a chemistry in our bunch that was synergistic which propelled us along as a group. I believe such was quite unusual for that day and age in that rural Southern setting. I have some theories as to why that was the case, which I'll save until another day. For now, suffice it to say, I'm proud to have been a member of that class.

It's been a long time since that day on April 16, 1959; our graduation day from PHS. Yes, as strange as it may seem, that's the correct date. Let me explain. After the school year began, the Board of Education eliminated "cotton pickin' " for the first time in forever. So, we graduated a month early enabling many of us to go to work sooner to either stash back some money to get ready for college or embark on our work careers.

In 1959, Barbie was introduced to the world. So was Fidel Castro. Strangely enough, they're both still going strong and looking about the same. On our senior trip, we saw Castro's motorcade to the United Nations building in New York City. He was being portrayed as a great liberator who had led a Cuban revolution and overthrown the corrupt Batista. The Castro motorcade brought cheers from some, jeers from others. The noisy protestors were handing out leaflets denouncing Castro. We thought they were radical nuts.

On our senior trip, we toured Washington, DC, New York City, and then went upstate to Niagra Falls. We spent two years making enough money to take that trip. For a group of kids from West Tennessee, most of whom had never been out of the state, that class trip was an education in itself.

In 1959, Alaska and Hawaii joined these United States. The Dodgers beat the White Sox in the World Series, Floyd Patterson was heavy weight champion of the world. Do you remember the top rated television program? Does this help? The sidekick was Chester, the starlet was Miss Kitty and Mr. Dillon was the main man. Yeah, it was *Gunsmoke*. It was actually the #1 rated television program from '57-'61. Incidently, I never did believe that Mr. Dillon and Miss Kitty were "just friends." The #1 song of 1959? Sung by Bobby Darrin. Still can't get it? *Mack the Knife*.

In 1959, a lot of Old Friends sallied forth to meet a brave new world– a world that has really changed.

➤

In These 45 Years...

Life really is different today,
   Than it was way back then.
Though we've gone in many directions
   In the class of '59 we've still got a friend.

   In These 45 Years...

Some times have been smooth,
And some others were rough;
Some years have been easy,
And others were tough.

   In These 45 Years...

Remembering life in the 50's,
   As for me, and I suspect for you,
Brings a great big smile,
   Because for me it's true;

Growing up in the small town of Parsons
   Was really quite good.
And I'd do it all over again,
   If I could, if I could... wouldn't you?!

           dd

➤

Closing the Guided Tour
of
Backtracking through the 50's

So, how do we close this feeble attempt at backtracking through the 50's? Believing (as I do) that endings are terribly important in nearly every aspect of life, means that I've always had trouble bringing things to a close. Par for the course, I've struggled with how to end this effort of reflecting on life in the 50's by a card-carrying, clinical member of that era.

Forgive me, but to put things in perspective, I must chase a rabbit for a bit. Several years ago, my brother, Mickey, decided he wanted a fireplace in the den of his house, and in typical Mickey fashion, he was determined to build it himself. Since he had never built a fireplace nor even laid any bricks, he went to the book store and bought two books– *How to Lay Bricks* and *How to Build a Fireplace*– and he did it. I mean he built a huge fireplace– a wall to wall job with a very large opening. When I saw it for the first time I was shocked at the magnitude of the project and the quality of the work. Knowing that I couldn't do something like that if my life depended on it, I hit him with one of those "Yes but.." responses. You know, like "Well, that's a good looking boat you've got there– but will it float?!" You know people like that, don't you? "Yeah, that's a great looking watch you bought, but let me show you a REAL watch." So, when I saw the extraordinary work that Mickey had done, I slipped into the, "yes but... mode."

Knowing that fireplaces are notorious for smoking up a room if they don't draw properly, I threw out my tacky "yes, but.." question. Well, that's an awesome job Mickey BUT will it draw?"

"Will it draw," he chimed, "the first time I built a fire in it, it sucked a sack of nails off the hearth!"

After a good laugh, I settled down and got over how jealous I was that he could do such a thing when I could not, and I asked another question that was much more appropriate than the first.

"Mickey, that really is a great piece of work and I'm proud of you for it, so, tell me, what was the hardest part of the entire job?" His answer to that question was equally as quick as the first one.

"The hardest part was deciding where to lay the first brick! The second one was easy– it only had two options."

Isn't that a great story? I thought you'd like that and would cut me some slack about chasing a rabbit with another story. But I really told it because it represents what went through my mind as I tried to bring this piece to an end. My conclusion was, I'd go back to where *Once Upon a Lifetime...* began– back to where I laid the first brick.

So, after much consternation, experimentation, and deletions, it occurred to me that the obvious place to end this tour is the same way all tours end– at the place they began. So, here goes–

The period that we call *The 50's* was actually more

a state of mind than *a place in time* and lasted longer
than the decade implies. Beginning sometime in the
late 40's, the 50's state of mind lasted until a deranged
sniper took a high powered rifle, went to a strategic
spot in the Book Depository Building in Dallas,
Texas, and in the blink of an eye snuffed out the life
of President John Fitzgerald Kennedy and ended the
50's state of mind– November 23, 1963.

The 50's were a great time to be alive and a great
time for growing up. However, the 50's were no
better than the 60's, 70's, 80's, 90's or the early years
of the 21st century. But, make no mistake about it–
life in the 50's was different than it is now. Very
different – shockingly different.

Can you handle one more glaring example? In the
50's *The Tonight Show* host, Jack Parr, was censored
for telling a joke in which he used the term "WC"
which stood for "water closet" a British phrase that
meant bathroom! During the Super Bowl of 2004,
pop singers, Janet Jackson and Justin Timberlake,
were censored because he tore off her blouse exposing
a naked breast to a worldwide television audience on
Sunday evening, prime time. Contrasting these two
t.v. experiences may say it as well as it can be stated–
things are different today than they were back then.

A couple of years ago, NBC news anchor, Tom
Brokaw, wrote a best selling book about the
generation that weathered the Great Depression and
stood tall during World War II. Entitled *The Greatest
Generation*, NBC's astute South Dakotan certainly

makes a good case for the extraordinary merits and virtues of that generation of Americans. But I'm not sure it's ever fair to measure one generation against another and certainly not fair to give one the title– "the greatest."

It is my guess that Brokaw succumbed to his own emotional prejudice because that was the generation of his parents and he was at a place in life to really appreciate the efforts and sacrifices they made on his behalf. Having parents from that period myself, I can certainly identify with his partiality. But I still take issue with comparing one generation with another on the grounds of merits and virtues. My reasoning is simple– I believe every generation in American history has produced greatness, splendor, and grandeur. Unfortunately, it's not often recognized while it's happening and only in retrospect do we truly understand the magnitude of each period of time. Then, when we finally do recognize it, we tend to idolize it and dramatize it, and yes, even embellish and enhance it. Doing so is fine as long as we don't fall into the exclusivity trap of revering a past generation and denigrating the younger and current generations.

Believing (as I do) that greatness has many ancestors and all of our successes are built on the backs and shoulders of many who have gone before us, I celebrate that each generation and every person in it, has the chance to take life to another level.

So, now I'm about to contradict myself which does

not bother me in the least because I believe that a great American poet and songwriter had me in mind without knowing it when he penned his classic song, *The Pilgrim*. Kris Kristofferson's song said:

He's a walking contradiction, partly truth and partly fiction, taking every wrong direction on his lonely way back home.

So, having confessed my contradictory ways, I will now state what I believe to be true regarding this issue. As an evolutionist in conviction and observation, my theory is– marriages are steadily improving and the good ones are **better** than they've ever been; parenting is steadily improving and good parents are **better** than they've ever been; enlightened and conscientious people are progressing and are **smarter** and **wiser** than they've ever been; and life in general is evolving and is **better** in 2004 than at any time in the history of this planet.

As I stated earlier, I know to some extent these statements are contradictions to my previous comments of displeasure about comparing one generation to another, regarding which generation is "greatest." But my position is: Each generation is different– not greater or lessor, just different, because the evolution of progress and the living of life demands a different response to the circumstances of the times. I'm not talking about "better" in terms of virtue, desire, or effort but "better" in terms of insight, progression, and truth; and, therefore, BETTER in clarity of purpose, passion for people, and efficiency of performance. Not better morally or ethically, nor in terms of endeavor but better in terms of the results, the outcome, the heritage and the legacy.

Perhaps an analogy will help clarify my point. It's amusing to me that sports enthusiasts are always asking how certain championship teams from the past compare with current winners. Could the Steelers of the 60's beat the Niners of the 80's? Would the Celtics of the 60's match up against the Bulls of the 90's? What about the Yankees of the 50's, could they play with the Yankees of the early 21st Century? Even though it makes for good conversational small-talk over beer and chips, such dialogue is really much ado about nothing. To those who view it rationally rather than emotionally, such comparisons are pointless because it's totally obvious that each generation of athletes is better than the one before– not "greater" in virtue, values, and integrity but "greater" in skills, knowledge, and performance.

To nail this point down with a twenty penny nail and a ball peen hammer, all you have to do is review the record books in track, swimming, snow skiing, speed skating and gymnastics. Each generation sets the bar higher than the one before. My conviction– the same is true in every aspect of life.

It is my prayer that God will keep us from falling into the trap of seeing only the flaws of today and not the merits. Yes, there are many things in our modern culture that need improvement– numerous things that need fixing– but life today is full of incredible opportunities, experiences, and virtues.

No matter which decade or generation identifies us, hopefully, we will look at our past histories honestly and openly, taking ownership for the shortcomings and celebrating the values and virtues of yesterday.

In the Prologue to this writing, I stated my conviction that the healthiest way to live life is with the maxim– *The Present is not the Past and Today is not Tomorrow*. Then I emphasized that the way to reach that position is to spend adequate time doing backward thinking and in so doing reliving and releasing the past. This short version of backtracking through the 50's has been my attempt to motivate you to do the same with the life and times of YOU.

Hearken to me, you who pursue deliverance, you who seek the Lord; look to the rock from which you were hewn, and to the quarry from which you were digged."

Isaiah 51:1

May we never forget from whence we came.

In Honor
of
Maxie & Zula Doyle
For their nurturing, guidance, and sacrifices
to help me grow up in the 50's!

(October 2003)

1958-59 Football Squad

Class of '59 Football Seniors

Back Row– L-R: Gerald Dickson, Olis Quinn, Bill Colwick,
Sam McIllwain, Jerry Wallace, Jimmy Jones
Front Row– L-R: Reuben Haggard, Bobby Myracle, Joe Houston,
Don Doyle, Tom Bawcum

Class of '59 Basketball Seniors

Back Row– L-R: Gerald Dickson, Oscar Spence, Bill Colwick,
Robert Canada, Larry Watson
Front Row– L-R: Tom Bawcum, Don Doyle, Jerry Wallace

'59 Senior Play Cast
"Hillbilly Wedding"
Directed by Leeburn Harris

"The Wedding"

"Ma" & "Pa"
Diane Tinker & Don Doyle

DFCC
110 Timber Creek Drive
Memphis, TN   38018

Director: Don Doyle, DMin, PhD
Associate: Matt Doyle, MS, LPC
Associate: Leanne Doyle Duncan, MS, LPC

Phones: 901/754-6214
          901/757-2347

Fax: 901/751-4140

email: dfcc@earthlink.net

Website: www.DFCC.net
➤

 The above data can be used to receive information regarding *The Doyle Family Counseling Center* and to order any of Don Doyle's books:

1. Heroes of the Heart
    Stories of Hurt, Hate, Horror, and Humor
2. Change is a Choice
    Common People Who Made Uncommon Choices
3. The Courage to Change Your Mind...
            Is the Power to Change Your Life
4. Once Upon a Lifetime...
            Backtracking Through the 50's